Exploring the crypto currency

Innovations, Challenges, and Future Trends

Series
Tech Industries — Insights and Perspectives Series

Mustafa Al-Dori

Copyright Page
Copyright © 2024 Mustafa Al-Dori. All rights reserved.

Dedication

For my parents, whose care, patience, and guidance helped shape who I am.

Acknowledgments

My sincere thanks to everyone who supported this book—my family, friends, mentors, and colleagues—for their encouragement and guidance. Thank you for being part of this journey.

Disclaimer

(Educational Purpose — Not Financial Advice)

This book is for education and general understanding. It does not provide financial, legal, tax, or investment advice. Cryptocurrency markets can be volatile, and digital assets can carry serious risks, including loss of funds.

Before making any decision, you should do your own research and, when needed, speak with a qualified professional in your country. Any examples in this book are for learning only. They are not recommendations to buy, sell, hold, or trade any asset.

About the Series

Tech Industries — Insights and Perspectives Series explains modern industries in clear, practical English. Each book in the series is designed to help you understand how a technology-driven field works, why it matters, and what risks and opportunities shape it.

The focus is always the same: real concepts, clean structure, and useful thinking tools. The goal is not to impress you with jargon. The goal is to help you see the industry as a system.

About This Book

Exploring the crypto currency: Innovations, Challenges, and Future Trends is a structured guide to the crypto world. It explains the technology, the market behavior, the real use cases, and the problems that slow adoption.

This book avoids hype and avoids fear. It gives you a calm way to think, so you can understand what is real, what is uncertain, and what depends on the country, the rules, and the time period.

How to Use This Book

You can read this book from start to finish, or you can use it like a tool. Each chapter begins with a short hook to frame the topic. Then it follows a consistent flow: definition, why it matters, how it works, a real example, common mistakes, and a quick check.

If you want speed, use the Reading Paths and the Quick Wins Map first. If you want deeper understanding, read the Foundations and Technology parts before the market sections. If you want safety, focus on security, scams, and verification habits early.

Reading Paths (3 Routes)

Route 1 — Beginner Clarity Path. Read the Foundations first, then Security and Scams, then the main Use Cases. This route builds a safe mental model before you face market noise.

Route 2 — Business and Strategy Path. Read Foundations, then Regulation and Compliance, then Use Cases, then Opportunities and Future Trends. This route helps you evaluate where crypto fits in real business.

Route 3 — Tech Understanding Path. Read Foundations, then Technology Layer, then Scaling and Infrastructure, then Security. This route helps you understand how the system works under the surface.

Quick Wins Map (1 Page)

If you only have one hour, start with the mental model in the Introduction. Then read the chapter that explains wallets, keys, and basic transactions. After that, read the security chapter and the scams chapter. These sections reduce the most common beginner risks. If you have one day, add the chapters on consensus, smart contracts, and project evaluation. This gives you the minimum structure needed to judge claims without guessing.

If you have one week, read the full book in order. Take the quick checks seriously. They are designed to turn reading into understanding.

Mini Glossary (Core Terms)

Blockchain. A shared record system that stores data in a way that is hard to change after confirmation.

Cryptocurrency. A digital asset that uses cryptography and a network to move value without a central operator.

Wallet. A tool that helps you manage keys and send or receive crypto. It is not always a "place" where coins are stored.

Address. A public identifier you share to receive crypto, similar to an account number.

Private Key. A secret that proves control over funds. If you lose it, recovery may be impossible.

Seed Phrase. A set of words that can restore a wallet. Anyone who has it can control the funds.

Transaction Fee. A cost paid to process a transaction. It often changes with network demand.

Exchange. A platform where users buy, sell, or swap assets. Some exchanges hold funds for you.

Custodial. A setup where a third party holds your keys and controls access to funds.

Non-custodial. A setup where you control your keys directly.

Stablecoin. A token designed to keep a stable price, often linked to a currency. Stability depends on its design and reserves.

Smart Contract. Code on a blockchain that can execute rules automatically under certain conditions.

Token. A digital unit issued on a blockchain, often representing access, utility, or value.

Consensus. The method a network uses to agree on the current state of the ledger.

Proof of Work. A consensus method that uses computational work to secure the network.

Proof of Stake. A consensus method that uses staked value and validator rules to secure the network.

DeFi. "Decentralized finance," meaning financial services built with smart contracts rather than traditional intermediaries.

NFT. A "non-fungible token," meaning a unique token that can represent ownership or membership in digital form.

Table of contents

Part 1 — Foundations Without Confusion	16
Chapter 1 — The Problem Crypto Tries to Solve	17
Chapter 2 — Crypto Basics You Must Know (No Jargon)	23
Chapter 3 — Blockchain Explained Like a Product	26
Part 2 — The Technology Layer (Clear and Practical)	31
Chapter 4 — Consensus Models and Security	32
Chapter 5 — Smart Contracts and Programmable Money	36
Chapter 6 — Scaling and Infrastructure	40
Part 3 — Markets, Trading, and Investing (Without the Hype)	44
Chapter 7 — How Crypto Markets Actually Move	45
Chapter 8 — Trading vs Investing vs Using	49
Chapter 9 — Project Evaluation Framework (The Reality Scorecard)	53
Part 4 — Regulation, Legal Reality, and Compliance	57
Chapter 10 — Regulation and Legal Challenges (Global View)	58
Chapter 11 — Taxes, Reporting, and Practical Compliance	63
Part 5 — Security, Scams, and Consumer Protection	67

Chapter 12 — Security for Real People	68
Chapter 13 — Scams, Fraud, and Market Manipulation	73
Part 6 — Real Applications and Industry Use Cases	77
Chapter 14 — Payments and Remittances	78
Chapter 15 — DeFi Without Buzzwords	82
Chapter 16 — NFTs and Digital Ownership (Beyond Art)	86
Chapter 17 — Tokenization and Real-World Assets	89
Chapter 18 — Enterprise and Government Uses	92
Part 7 — Challenges and Opportunities (Strategic Lens)	94
Chapter 19 — The Biggest Challenges Facing Crypto	96
Chapter 20 — Opportunities in the Digital Currency Market	100
Part 8 — Future Trends (Practical Forecasting)	104
Chapter 21 — Future of Digital Currencies (2026–2035)	105
Chapter 22 — A Calm Conclusion: How to Stay Smart	110

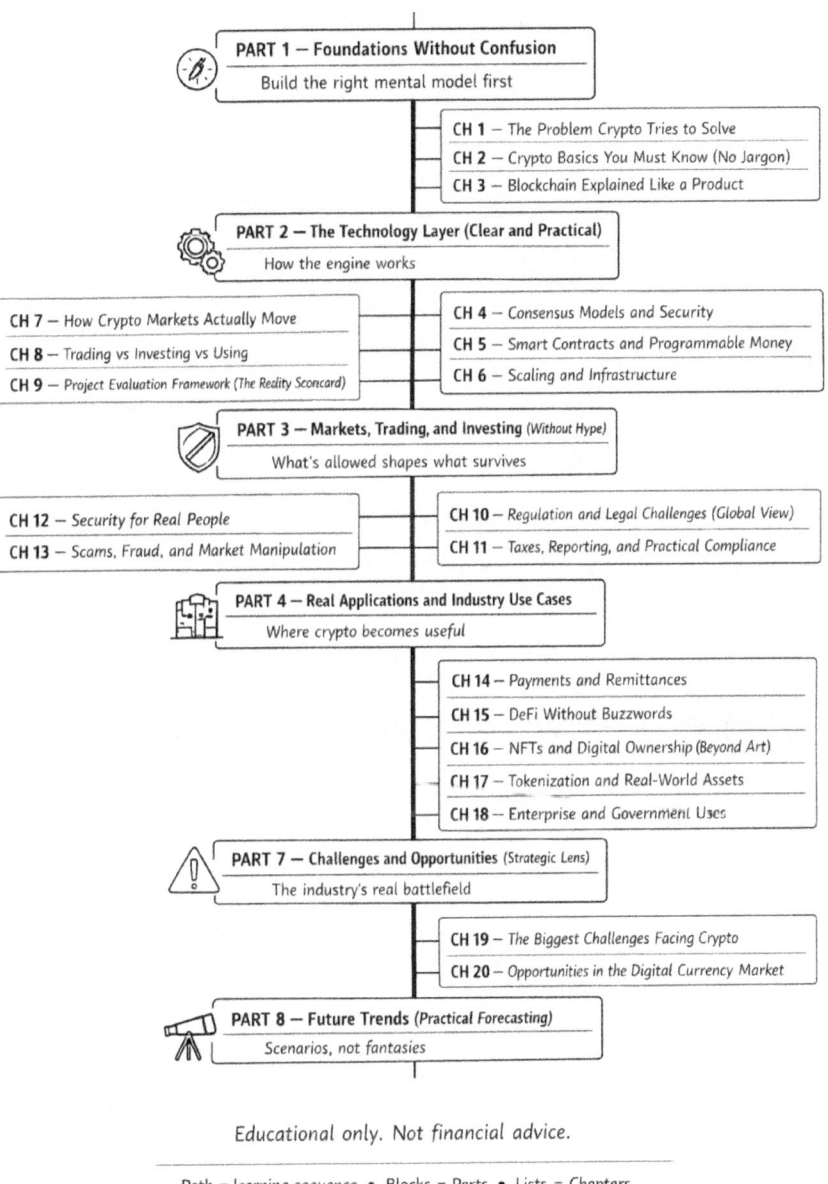

Exploring the Cryptocurrency
Innovations, Challenges, and Future Trends

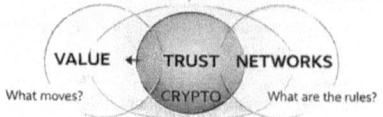

VALUE ← TRUST → NETWORKS
CRYPTO
What moves? What are the rules?

A system, not a slogan. A guide to thinking, not hype.

Introduction

Why Crypto Matters (Without Noise)

Crypto is often presented as a fight between believers and critics. That framing is loud, emotional, and rarely helpful. A calmer view is more useful: crypto is a set of tools that tries to move value in a world that is already digital. People send messages instantly, but moving money can still be slow, expensive, or limited by borders and banking hours. Crypto matters because it challenges that gap. It proposes new ways to transfer value, record ownership, and build trust between strangers without relying on a single central operator.

At the same time, crypto can be a magnet for hype. Prices move fast, opinions become extreme, and marketing can sound like certainty. This book does not ask you to love crypto or hate it. It asks you to understand it. Understanding gives you a stable base. It helps you separate useful ideas from risky behavior, and it helps you spot claims that do not match reality.

What This Book Is (and Isn't)

This book is a clear, structured guide to the crypto currency world. It explains the foundations, the technology layer, the market dynamics, the real use cases, and the risks that often harm beginners. It also explores regulation, security, common scam patterns, and practical ways to verify information. The goal is to help you think and act with discipline, not emotion.

This book is not financial advice. It does not tell you what to buy or when to sell. It does not promise profit, and it does not treat risk as a small detail. It also avoids the false idea that crypto is "the future of everything." Some crypto projects may succeed, some may fail, and many will change. In several areas, the honest answer is "it depends," because rules, adoption, and technology evolve across countries and over time.

A Simple Mental Model: Value + Trust + Networks

To understand crypto without getting lost, you need a simple mental model. Here it is: crypto sits at the intersection of value, trust, and networks. Value is what people want to store, move, or exchange. Trust is the reason people accept a transaction as real and final. Networks are the systems that connect people and enforce shared rules.

Traditional money systems often place trust in institutions. Banks, payment companies, and regulators play that role. Crypto tries a different method. It uses cryptography, shared ledgers, and network rules to create trust through verification rather than permission. This does not remove human trust entirely, because people still trust software, platforms, and sometimes stablecoin issuers. But it shifts where trust lives and how it is enforced.

When you read anything about crypto, ask three questions through this model. What kind of value is being moved or stored. How trust is created or protected. Which network rules make the system work, and what happens when those rules are tested. This mental model will help you avoid getting trapped in slogans.

How to Read This Book Like a System

You can read this book in order, but you can also read it as a system. A system has parts, trade-offs, and failure points. If you start with price talk, you may miss the real structure. That is why the early chapters focus on foundations. They give you the language and the logic you need before you face market noise.

Each chapter follows the same flow. First, it defines the concept in clear English. Then it explains why the concept matters. Next, it shows how it works in practice. After that, it gives a real example, because examples turn ideas into understanding. Then it highlights common mistakes, because mistakes are where money and trust are often lost. Finally, it ends with a quick check. The quick check is small, but it is important. If you can answer it, you did not just read. You learned.

Quick Check: 7 Questions to Ensure Clarity

1. Can I explain, in one short paragraph, what problem crypto is trying to solve.

2. Do I understand the difference between value, trust, and the network rules behind a crypto system.

3. Can I describe what a wallet does, without saying it "stores coins" in a confusing way.

4. Do I know what I control in crypto, and what I delegate to a platform or an exchange.

5. When I hear a claim, do I ask "how is this verified" before I ask "how much can I make."

6. Can I name two real risks that exist even when the technology works as designed.

7. Do I accept that some answers depend on country rules and time, and that certainty is not always honest.

Part 1 — Foundations Without Confusion

Part Introduction: Build the right mental model first

Before you can judge crypto, you need a clean mental model. Most confusion comes from skipping the basics and jumping straight to prices, predictions, and opinions. This part keeps things simple on purpose. It gives you the core ideas that everything else depends on, in plain English and in the right order.

You will start with the real problem crypto tries to solve. Money is not only numbers. It is a trust system. When trust is slow, expensive, or limited by borders, people feel friction. You will see why that friction exists, and what Bitcoin changed in a practical way. You will also learn which popular myths create false confidence or unnecessary fear.

Next, you will build your essential vocabulary without jargon. You will learn the difference between a coin and a token, what a wallet truly does, and why private keys matter. You will also understand transactions, confirmations, and fees as simple trade-offs inside a network.

Finally, you will study blockchain as if it were a product. You will see how shared records work, how networks agree through consensus, and what "immutability" really means. You will also learn why transparency and privacy are not the same thing, and why both matter.

If you master this part, the rest of the book becomes easier, calmer, and more honest.

Chapter 1 — The Problem Crypto Tries to Solve

Opening

The first time someone sends money across borders, they often expect a simple story. They press "send," and the money should arrive. Instead, the story becomes complicated. A fee appears that was not obvious at the start. A transfer that sounded quick becomes slow. The receiver gets less than expected. The sender tries to ask why, but the answer is not clear. The system feels like a black box. Crypto began as a response to this kind of frustration. It asked a direct question. What if digital value could move with clearer rules and fewer hidden steps.

Definition: What problem is crypto trying to solve

Crypto tries to solve a trust problem inside digital value. The internet can copy data perfectly. That is excellent for information. It is a problem for money. Money needs scarcity. It needs a reliable rule that prevents double spending. Double spending means using the same unit twice. In a simple digital file, copying is easy. For value, copying would break the system. Traditional finance solves this by placing trust in institutions. Banks and payment networks keep the ledger. A ledger is simply a record of who owns what and who paid whom. Crypto proposes another way to maintain that ledger and protect scarcity. It uses shared records and verification rules so that trust can be created through checks, not only through permission.

Trust gaps in money and digital value

Money is a social agreement. It works because people expect others to accept it later. In many countries, this trust is supported by laws, institutions, and long habits. That structure can be strong. It can also create gaps. Some people are excluded from banking because of location, paperwork, or cost. Some users face delays because systems depend on business hours. Some payments are blocked by risk rules or geopolitical constraints. Some cross-border transfers involve multiple intermediaries. Each intermediary can add cost and time. This is not always evil. These steps often exist to reduce fraud and enforce rules. The problem is that the user experience can feel unpredictable. People may not know who is holding the funds, why a delay happened, or what the final cost will be. That uncertainty is a trust gap.

Digital value adds another layer of difficulty. In the digital world, ownership is often managed by platforms. A platform can update records in a database. A user trusts that platform to keep the record correct and to treat users fairly. This is common in online banking and also in social apps and gaming economies. The platform model can be efficient. It can also create single points of failure. If the platform freezes an account, changes rules, or is hacked, the user may have limited control. Crypto asks whether ownership records can be shared across many participants, so no single party can quietly rewrite the history. This is not a perfect solution. It is a different design with different risks.

Why traditional systems create friction

Friction is the cost of coordination and risk management. Traditional finance is built to handle disputes, fraud, compliance, and customer protection. That work requires checks. It requires reporting. It requires identity verification. It requires monitoring. These functions are important. They also add steps. When money stays inside one local system, those steps can be hidden and fast. When money crosses systems, the steps become visible. Different countries have different banks, different rules, different currencies, and different settlement processes. A cross-border payment can pass through several entities.

Each entity can apply a fee. Each entity can apply a rate. Each entity can require additional review. Some of this friction reduces risk. Some of it exists because systems were built at different times and must still work together.

Friction also comes from the difference between "message speed" and "settlement speed." A bank can send a message quickly that a payment is planned. Final settlement can still take time. Settlement is the moment ownership is fully updated and cannot be undone under normal conditions. Many users do not separate these concepts. They see a notification and think the transfer is done. That mismatch creates frustration. It also creates business problems. A supplier may wait for confirmation. A worker may wait for wages. A family may wait for support money. The waiting has a real cost, even if the system is doing what it was designed to do.

What Bitcoin changed (in plain English)

Bitcoin introduced a new method for digital scarcity and shared agreement. It created a system where many participants can hold the same ledger and can agree on updates through a defined process. This process is called consensus. Consensus means agreement. In a blockchain, it means agreement on which transactions are valid and in what order. Bitcoin's design made it possible for strangers to coordinate without trusting a central ledger manager to act fairly. Instead, the network verifies transactions using rules. The ledger becomes public and shared. Updates become hard to change after confirmation. This property is often called immutability. Immutability does not mean "impossible to change." It means "very hard to rewrite history without breaking the rules or controlling the system." The strength of that property depends on the network design.

Bitcoin also introduced a practical concept of digital ownership through keys. The system does not need your name to function. It needs proof that you control the keys linked to an address. That is why crypto can feel different from banking. In many crypto systems, control is linked to key management rather than identity accounts. This can enable open access. It can also create responsibility that many users are not ready for. If you control the keys, you control the funds. If you lose the keys, recovery may be impossible. Bitcoin did not solve every payment problem. It changed the trust architecture. That change inspired many other systems.

How it works at a high level

At a high level, a crypto network keeps a ledger. Users create transactions. Transactions follow rules. The network checks them. Valid transactions are added to the ledger. The ledger is shared across many participants, so verification is distributed. This can reduce dependence on a single gatekeeper. It can also introduce trade-offs. Public verification can reduce privacy. Distributed coordination can reduce speed. Security can require costs. Every design choice produces a different mix of benefits and problems. That is why crypto is not one product. It is a category of designs.

Real example: an everyday use case without hype

Consider a remote worker who earns money from international clients. The worker needs a method to receive value reliably. Traditional options may include bank transfers or payment companies. These can work well, but fees and delays can still be painful. In some cases, the worker may not have access to the same services as clients in another country. The worker may explore a stablecoin. A stablecoin is a token designed to keep a stable price, often linked to a currency. This approach can be faster in some situations, but it introduces new questions. Which platform will convert the funds. What are the local rules. What are the platform risks. What happens if the service pauses withdrawals. The crypto option offers a new rail. It does not remove risk. It moves risk into different places. This example shows the real problem crypto targets. It is not only speed. It is optionality, access, and transparency of rules.

Mini Case: sending money across borders

Imagine a small business owner paying a supplier abroad. The owner sends funds through a bank. The bank sends the payment through partners. The supplier waits. The bank cannot always predict the exact arrival time. The supplier may also receive less because conversion and fees are applied along the path. The business owner experiences uncertainty. Now imagine the owner tries a crypto route. The owner converts to a digital asset and sends it. The network transfer may be quick. The supplier can often see the transaction status on the public ledger. That visibility can reduce uncertainty. Yet the business now faces other risks. The conversion step depends on service providers. The business must manage keys or trust custody. Fees can change with network congestion. Local compliance may require reporting. The lesson is not that crypto is always better. The lesson is that crypto is a response to pain points in coordination, access, and transparency. It offers a different toolset.

Common myths that confuse beginners

A common myth is that crypto removes trust. It does not. It changes how trust is built. People may trust code, validators, miners, exchanges, wallet apps, and stablecoin issuers. Another myth is that crypto is always anonymous. Many blockchains are transparent. Anyone can often see transactions. Privacy depends on the network and the user. Another myth is that crypto transactions are always cheap and instant. Fees and speed depend on design and demand. Another myth is that "decentralized" automatically means safe. Decentralization can reduce single points of control. It does not prevent scams, bugs, or user mistakes. A final myth is that learning crypto is mainly learning charts. Charts show behavior. They do not explain the system. If you start with charts, you may learn stress rather than understanding.

Quick Check

Can you explain, in your own words, what "trust" means in a money system.

Can you name two reasons cross-border transfers can feel slow or unclear.

Can you describe what Bitcoin changed without talking about price.

Can you list one myth that could lead a beginner into a bad decision.

Can you explain why a "faster path" may still include new kinds of risk.

Chapter 2 — Crypto Basics You Must Know (No Jargon)

Opening

Most crypto mistakes happen before people even "do" anything. They happen when someone uses the wrong words and carries the wrong picture in their head. If you think a wallet is a bank account, you will expect bank-account safety. If you think a transaction is like an email, you will ignore finality and fees. If you think "private key" is a password you can reset, you will take risks you cannot undo. This chapter gives you the minimum language you need to think clearly. It stays simple on purpose, because confusion is expensive.

Coin vs token (practical difference)

A coin is a cryptocurrency that belongs to its own network. It is the native asset that the network uses for basic operations, such as paying fees and securing activity. A token is a digital unit created on top of an existing network. It uses that network's rules rather than running its own network from scratch. In practice, coins are often tied to the health and design of a specific blockchain. Tokens are often tied to a project, an application, or a set of rules written as code. The word "token" does not automatically mean risky. It simply means the asset lives on another platform.

Wallets, addresses, and private keys

A wallet is a tool that helps you control access to crypto. It manages your keys and helps you send and receive transactions. A wallet is not always a "place" where coins are stored. Coins are recorded on the blockchain. The wallet is the interface that proves you have the right to move them. An address is a public identifier you share to receive crypto. It is similar to an account number, but it does not prove ownership by itself. The private key is the secret that proves control. If someone has your private key, they can usually move your funds. If you lose it and you have no backup, recovery may be impossible. Some wallets also give a seed phrase, which is a set of words that can restore your wallet. A seed phrase must be treated like a master key, because it can unlock everything.

Transactions and confirmations

A transaction is a signed instruction that moves value from one address to another. "Signed" means it includes cryptographic proof that the sender has control. After a transaction is created, it is broadcast to the network. The network does not accept it instantly as final in most cases. It is processed, checked against rules, and then included in a block. A confirmation means the network has accepted the transaction into the shared record. More confirmations usually mean stronger confidence that the transaction will not be reversed. Finality is the point where reversal becomes extremely unlikely or not allowed by the network's design. Finality depends on the blockchain and its consensus method, so you should not assume the same behavior everywhere.

Fees and why they exist

Fees exist because networks have limited space and limited processing capacity. When many people send transactions at the same time, the network needs a way to prioritize. Fees also reward the participants who run the network and process transactions, depending on the network model. Fees can change. They often rise when demand is high and fall when demand is lower. This is why a "cheap network" can become expensive during congestion. Fees are not only a cost. They can also be a signal of demand, competition for space, and the health of network activity.

Common mistakes

A common mistake is treating a wallet like a bank account and assuming someone will restore access if something goes wrong. In many non-custodial setups, nobody can reset your password. Another mistake is sharing a seed phrase or storing it in an unsafe place, such as an online note or a screenshot. A third mistake is sending funds on the wrong network or to an incompatible address format. That error can lead to permanent loss, depending on the situation. Another mistake is ignoring fees, especially during busy periods, and then being surprised by delays or higher costs. A final mistake is trusting labels like "official" without verification, which makes users vulnerable to fake apps and phishing links.

Quick Check

Can you explain the difference between a coin and a token in one short paragraph.
Can you describe what a wallet does without saying it "stores coins" as if it were a bank.
Do you understand why a private key or seed phrase must never be shared.
Can you explain what a confirmation means, and why more confirmations can matter.
Can you give one clear reason fees can rise, even if the network is "working."

Chapter 3 — Blockchain Explained Like a Product

Opening

Many people treat blockchain like a magic word. They hear it and assume something is automatically modern, safe, and unstoppable. Others hear it and assume it is automatically a scam. Both reactions skip the same step. They skip understanding. The simplest way to understand blockchain is to treat it like a product. A product has a purpose, a design, trade-offs, and failure points. When you see blockchain this way, you stop arguing about labels. You start asking practical questions. What does it record. Who can write to it. Who can read it. How does it handle mistakes. What does it cost to use. What must stay true for it to remain trustworthy.

Blocks and shared records

A blockchain is a shared record system. The shared record is called a ledger. A ledger is a history of transactions and state changes. "Shared" means many participants keep a copy. Each participant can check whether new updates follow the rules. This shared setup is different from a private database controlled by one company. In a private database, one operator can change the record. The operator may still be honest and secure, but the control is centralized. In a blockchain, control is distributed across participants who follow a common protocol. A protocol is a set of rules for how the system works and how participants communicate.

The term "block" is simply a way to package updates. A block is a batch of transactions or events that the network agrees to add to the ledger. Blocks are linked in order, forming a chain. That link is done through cryptographic references. You do not need to know the math to get the idea. The reference makes it difficult to change a past block without causing a mismatch later. This is why people say blockchain is "tamper resistant." It is designed to make rewriting history hard, not to make mistakes impossible.

A shared ledger solves one key problem. It creates a single agreed history without needing one central owner. That can be useful when many parties need the same truth, and no single party is trusted to control it alone. But sharing also creates costs. A shared system is often slower than a private system. A shared system can be more transparent than users expect. A shared system also needs a strong method for agreement, or it becomes chaos. That method is consensus.

Consensus: how agreement happens

Consensus is how the network agrees on what is true. It answers a simple question: which transactions are valid, and in what order. Without consensus, participants might disagree. One group might accept one history. Another group might accept a different history. That would break the idea of a shared ledger.

There are different consensus methods. You have already seen the names Proof of Work and Proof of Stake. You do not need to master them yet, but you need the principle. Consensus is a rule-based process that makes it costly or difficult to cheat. It also gives the network a way to handle competing claims about the ledger. A good consensus method helps the network resist attacks, maintain uptime, and recover from problems. A weak consensus method can lead to instability or manipulation.

Consensus also explains why blockchains have limits. Agreement takes coordination. Coordination takes time and resources. When more people use a network at the same time, the network must still keep agreement. If it tries to accept everything instantly, it can lose reliability. Many networks choose reliability over raw speed. This is why blockchains often trade speed for trust. It is also why new designs focus on scaling. Scaling means improving capacity without losing security or decentralization.

Immutability: what it means (and doesn't)

Immutability is one of the most misunderstood blockchain words. It does not mean that data can never change. It means that once a block is confirmed and deeply embedded in the chain, changing it becomes very difficult under the rules of the system. In many networks, rewriting old history would require controlling a large portion of the network's security resources. That is not always impossible in theory. It is often impractical in well-secured networks.

Immutability is not a moral guarantee. It does not mean the data is true. If someone writes false information into a blockchain, the blockchain will not correct it by itself. It will store what it was given. Immutability protects the record from silent editing. It does not protect the record from bad inputs. This is important when people talk about real-world assets, identity, or certificates on a blockchain. The chain can preserve the record. It cannot prove that the record matched reality when it was created. Reality needs verification outside the chain. That is why oracles and audits matter, and why governance matters.

Immutability also has a user-side cost. In many systems, if you send funds to the wrong address, the network may not reverse it. The network is following rules. It does not know your intention. This can feel harsh, but it is consistent with the design. Some systems build additional layers for recovery and customer protection. Those layers can help usability. They can also reintroduce trust in intermediaries. Again, blockchain is a product with trade-offs, not a free miracle.

Transparency vs privacy

Another confusing area is the difference between transparency and privacy. Many public blockchains are transparent by design. That means the ledger can be viewed by anyone. Transactions can be inspected. Balances tied to addresses can often be traced. This transparency can improve auditability. It can also create privacy concerns. Many users assume crypto is private because they do not see names on the ledger. But privacy is not only about names. Privacy is about whether activity can be linked to a person through patterns, exchanges, or identity checks.

Some networks and tools aim to increase privacy. Others aim to increase compliance visibility. Many systems sit in the middle. The key point is that privacy is not automatic. It is a design choice and an operational behavior. If you use a service that requires identity verification, your address activity may be linkable to you within that service. If you reuse addresses or expose your address publicly, others may track your activity more easily. If you use a hardware wallet and good operational habits, you may reduce some exposure. Still, there is no single rule. Privacy depends on the network, the tools, and the user's choices.

When you evaluate a blockchain product, treat transparency as a feature with costs. Transparency can help detect fraud and prove payments. It can also expose business flows and personal habits. Businesses may want selective privacy. Individuals may want privacy for safety. Regulators may want transparency for enforcement. These goals can conflict. That is why "privacy vs transparency" is not a simple debate. It is a system design tension.

One-page explanation

A blockchain is a shared ledger that records transactions and state changes. Instead of one company controlling the database, many participants keep copies and verify updates. Updates are grouped into blocks. Blocks are linked in order to form a history that is hard to rewrite silently. The network uses a consensus method to agree on which updates are valid and what order they happened in. This agreement process is what gives the ledger its shared truth.

Immutability means confirmed history is difficult to change under the rules. It does not mean the information is automatically correct. It protects records from hidden edits, not from false inputs. Transparency means many ledgers are visible to the public. This can increase auditability but can reduce privacy. Privacy depends on the network design, the tools used, and user behavior. A blockchain is useful when many parties need a shared record without trusting one central controller. It can be less useful when speed, low cost, or private data are the top priorities.

The practical takeaway is simple. Blockchain is not magic. It is a product design. It trades some speed and simplicity for shared verification and resistance to silent changes. When you hear a blockchain claim, ask four questions. What is being recorded. Who can write updates. How does the network agree. What happens when something goes wrong.

Quick Check

Can you explain what a ledger is in plain English.
Can you describe what a block is without using technical math.
Can you explain consensus as "how a network agrees" in one paragraph.
Can you explain immutability as "hard to rewrite," not "impossible."
Can you describe one benefit and one cost of transparency.
Can you explain why a blockchain record can still contain false inputs.
Can you state one case where a private database may be a better choice.

Part 2 — The Technology Layer (Clear and Practical)

Part Introduction: how the engine works

In Part 1, you built the mental model. In Part 2, you learn how the engine actually runs. This matters because many crypto arguments are really technology arguments in disguise. People talk about speed, cost, safety, and "trust," but they often mix the terms. When you understand the engine, you can separate what is a design choice from what is a temporary problem. You can also spot when a claim ignores a trade-off.

This part explains three practical layers. First, it explains consensus and security, which is how a network agrees on truth and protects itself from cheating. Second, it explains smart contracts, which turn a blockchain from a payment rail into a programmable platform. Third, it explains scaling and infrastructure, which is how networks grow without breaking trust.

You do not need to be a developer to understand this. You just need clean definitions and a product mindset. You will learn what "finality" means in plain English. You will learn why attacks happen and what they target. You will learn why smart contracts can be powerful and dangerous at the same time. You will learn why congestion happens and what Layer 2 is trying to fix. By the end of Part 2, you should be able to read technical claims calmly and ask better questions before you trust a system with value.

Chapter 4 — Consensus Models and Security

Opening

When people say a blockchain is "secure," they often mean "I trust it." That is not a security definition. Security is not a feeling. Security is a set of conditions that make cheating difficult. It is also a set of costs that attackers must pay to break rules. This chapter explains the basic security story of crypto networks. It shows how a network agrees on the truth, when a transaction is truly done, and how attacks work in simple terms. It also addresses the energy debate in a calm way, without turning it into a political argument.

Definition: what consensus and security mean

Consensus is the method a network uses to agree on the state of the ledger. The ledger is the shared record. Security is the network's ability to resist invalid changes to that record. In simple terms, consensus decides what counts as a valid update. Security makes it hard to push invalid updates through. Most security discussions in crypto are really discussions about incentives, costs, and coordination. A system is secure when honest behavior is easier and cheaper than cheating, and when attacks require resources that are hard to obtain or hard to keep.

Proof of Work vs Proof of Stake (trade-offs)

Proof of Work is a consensus model where participants compete by performing computational work. The network accepts the work as evidence that real resources were spent. This work helps defend the network because rewriting history would require repeating large amounts of work. Proof of Work tends to be simple in concept and strong in its "cost to rewrite" story. It also introduces costs that are visible, such as energy use and specialized hardware. Those costs are part of what makes attacks expensive. They are not only waste. They are also the price of the security design.

Proof of Stake is a consensus model where participants lock value inside the system and earn the right to validate updates under rules. Instead of proving "work," they prove "stake," meaning they have something to lose if they cheat. If validators break rules, they may be punished by the protocol, depending on the design. Proof of Stake often aims to reduce energy costs and increase flexibility. It also changes the security discussion. The key question becomes how stake is distributed, how validators are selected, and how the system handles coordination risks. Proof of Stake can work well, but its security is tied to governance, incentives, and the behavior of large stakeholders.

The trade-off is not "good vs bad." The trade-off is "which risks you accept." Proof of Work accepts high resource use as part of its security model. Proof of Stake accepts a model where economic stake and governance design play a stronger role. Both can be attacked in different ways. Both can also be defended well when the system is designed and operated with discipline.

Finality: when a transaction is "done"

Finality is the moment a transaction becomes effectively irreversible under normal conditions. Many beginners assume that "sent" means "done." In crypto networks, there is often a process. A transaction is created and broadcast. Then it is included in a block. Then additional blocks are added after it. Each step increases confidence that the network will not replace that history with a different version.

Some systems aim for strong finality faster. Some systems have probabilistic finality, meaning confidence increases over time. The details depend on the network design. You do not need to memorize every model. You need one habit. Do not treat a transaction as final only because you see it on a screen. Treat it as final when the network's confirmation standard is satisfied for your risk level. Higher value transfers deserve stronger confirmation habits. Business transfers deserve even more discipline, because disputes cost more than fees.

Attacks explained simply

Most attacks aim at one of three targets. The first target is consensus, meaning the attacker tries to influence what the network accepts as true. This can include attempts to rewrite recent history or exclude certain transactions. The second target is software, meaning the attacker exploits bugs in clients, nodes, or smart contracts. The third target is humans, meaning the attacker uses phishing, fake apps, and social engineering to steal keys or approvals.

A common fear is the idea that an attacker can "hack the blockchain" in one dramatic moment. Real attacks are usually more practical and less cinematic. An attacker looks for weak points. A weak point can be low network security, poorly designed incentives, concentrated validator power, or rushed code. It can also be careless users. In many cases, the easiest attack is not breaking consensus. The easiest attack is tricking people into giving up access.

This is why you should separate network security from user security. A network can be strong, but users can still lose funds. A protocol can be correct, but a wallet app can be fake. A smart contract can be well-known, but a phishing link can redirect approvals. Security is layered. The strongest layer does not cancel the weaker ones.

Energy debate: facts vs claims

Energy use is often presented as a moral verdict. That framing hides the technical truth. Some consensus models use energy as part of security. The question is not only "how much energy." The question is "what security role does that energy play, and what alternatives cost instead."

Alternatives may reduce energy but introduce other costs or risks, such as stronger dependence on governance design or validator concentration.

It is also important to avoid absolute claims. Energy profiles differ across networks and over time. The electricity source mix can vary by region. Reliable public measurement can be difficult, and many statements online are simplified for debate rather than for learning. The honest approach is to treat energy as one trade-off among many. A serious evaluation compares security benefits, environmental concerns, system utility, and available alternatives. This book does not ask you to pick a side. It asks you to understand what the debate is actually about.

Quick Check

Can you explain consensus as "how a network agrees on truth."
Can you describe the difference between Proof of Work and Proof of Stake as a trade-off.
Can you explain finality as "when done really means done."
Can you name the three broad targets of attacks: consensus, software, and humans.
Can you explain why energy use is tied to design choices, not just politics.

Chapter 5 — Smart Contracts and Programmable Money

Opening

A basic blockchain can move value from one address to another. That is useful, but it is limited. Smart contracts changed the category because they introduced programmable rules. They made it possible to build markets, loans, swaps, and digital ownership systems without a traditional operator running the logic. This sounds powerful, and it is. It is also risky, because code can fail, and code can be exploited. This chapter explains what smart contracts are, what they can and cannot do, and why "programmable money" must be handled with maturity.

Definition: what a smart contract is

A smart contract is code stored and executed on a blockchain. It follows rules that are visible and repeatable. When conditions are met, the contract can update balances, move tokens, or change recorded state. In many systems, the contract's behavior is deterministic. Deterministic means the same inputs should produce the same outputs. This predictability is a key reason smart contracts are useful. The contract does not need to "trust" a company employee to run it honestly. It runs according to the code, as long as the network accepts the execution.

What smart contracts can and can't do

Smart contracts can automate rules inside the blockchain environment. They can hold assets, enforce conditions, and coordinate multiple parties without a central controller. They can support decentralized exchanges, lending pools, and membership systems. They can also create complex token behavior, such as locking, vesting, and governance votes.

Smart contracts cannot directly know real-world truth by themselves. A contract cannot see a weather report, a court decision, a shipping event, or a company balance sheet unless that information is brought into the blockchain in a trusted way. Smart contracts also cannot protect you from poor design. If a contract allows a dangerous action, and you trigger it, the chain may treat it as valid. Contracts also cannot guarantee fairness. A contract can be "fair" in code but still create unfair outcomes if the rules are biased or if users do not understand them.

Token standards and rules

Tokens often follow standards. A standard is a common interface that helps wallets, exchanges, and applications handle tokens consistently. Standards reduce friction because tools can support many tokens with the same basic logic. Standards also create predictable behavior, but predictable does not mean safe. A token can follow a standard and still be a bad product. The most important rule is not "does it follow a standard." The important rule is "what does this token allow, and who controls those permissions."

Some tokens are designed to be fixed-supply. Some can be minted, meaning new units can be created under rules. Some can be frozen, meaning transfers can be blocked by a controller. Some can be upgraded through governance or a developer-controlled process. None of these features are automatically good or bad. They are design choices. As a reader, your job is to see the choices and understand their consequences.

Oracles: connecting to real world data

An oracle is a mechanism that brings external information into the blockchain environment. This might include price feeds, interest rates, event outcomes, or other data. Oracles matter because many smart contracts depend on real-world inputs. A lending contract might need a price to decide collateral value. A derivatives contract might need an index level. Without oracles, smart contracts are trapped in a closed world.

Oracles also introduce trust. If the oracle is wrong, delayed, manipulated, or unavailable, the contract can behave badly even if the contract code is correct. This is why oracle design is often a major risk factor. Good systems use redundancy, careful incentives, and clear failure handling. Poor systems rely on weak inputs and become easy to exploit.

Where smart contracts fail

Smart contracts fail in a few common ways. They can fail because of bugs. Bugs are logic mistakes that were not intended. They can fail because of poor assumptions, such as assuming a token behaves in a normal way when it has a special feature. They can fail because of integration risk, meaning the contract interacts with another contract that changes behavior or is compromised. They can fail because of oracle issues, where a wrong price or delayed update triggers wrong outcomes. They can also fail because users approve dangerous permissions without understanding what they signed.

A key lesson is this. Smart contracts remove some types of human discretion, but they do not remove human risk. They shift risk from "people making discretionary decisions" to "people writing rules and people using tools." That can be safer in some cases. It can be worse in others. Safety depends on design quality, review quality, and user behavior.

Mini Case: exploit lessons

Imagine a simple contract that allows users to deposit tokens and receive a reward. The contract also allows an "admin" function to update reward rules. A project launches quickly and attracts users. Later, a bug is discovered, or the admin key is compromised, or the oracle price feed behaves strangely. The result is the same from the user's view. Funds may be drained, rewards may become meaningless, or withdrawals may pause. The lesson is not "never use smart contracts." The lesson is to treat every contract like a financial machine. You want to know who controls upgrades, how risks are handled, what dependencies exist, and what happens in a failure.

In practice, many users skip these questions because the interface feels friendly. The interface can be a trap. A polished interface does not prove safe code. A large online community does not prove safe incentives. A confident influencer does not prove safe risk management. The contract only proves what it enforces, and the ecosystem around it decides whether the system stays healthy.

Quick Check

Can you define a smart contract as "code that runs on-chain under rules."
Can you explain one thing a smart contract can do and one thing it cannot do.
Can you explain why standards help tools but do not guarantee safety.
Can you define an oracle as "a bridge for external data," and name its risk.
Can you name two ways smart contracts fail: bugs, oracles, permissions, or integration risk.

Chapter 6 — Scaling and Infrastructure

Opening

A good crypto network can feel smooth when few people use it. Then a busy period arrives and everything changes. Fees rise. Transactions slow down. Users complain, and critics declare the technology finished. This pattern is normal for shared systems with limited capacity. Scaling is the effort to grow capacity without breaking trust. Infrastructure is the set of tools and layers that make the network usable in real life. This chapter explains congestion, the Layer 1 and Layer 2 idea, bridges, and why wallets are often the real adoption bottleneck.

Definition: what scaling means in crypto

Scaling means increasing the number of transactions and useful actions a system can handle while keeping security and reliability strong. In blockchain systems, scaling is hard because the system is shared. Many participants must verify updates. Verification is what gives trust. If you push capacity too far without care, you can reduce the ability of participants to verify, which can reduce decentralization and increase risk.

Why networks get congested

Congestion happens when demand for block space exceeds supply. Block space is the capacity inside blocks to include transactions or contract actions. When too many users compete at once, the network must choose what gets processed first. Many networks use fees as a prioritization tool. Higher fees often get faster inclusion. When demand drops, fees often fall. This is not always pleasant, but it is a predictable result of scarcity.

Congestion is also affected by what people are doing. A simple transfer may use fewer resources than a complex smart contract action. Heavy activity in popular applications can increase demand sharply. This is why the user experience can change fast. The network is not necessarily "broken." It is saturated.

Layer 1 vs Layer 2

Layer 1 is the base blockchain. It is the main network where consensus happens and where the ledger is secured. Layer 2 is a system built on top of Layer 1 to improve speed and cost, while still relying on Layer 1 for final settlement and security guarantees. Layer 2 designs vary, but the core goal is the same. Move more activity off the base layer, then settle results back to the base layer in a secure way.

A useful mental model is this. Layer 1 is the court of record. Layer 2 is a faster processing lane that reports back to the court. If Layer 2 is well-designed, you get better user experience without losing the trust anchor. If Layer 2 is poorly designed, you may get speed but carry hidden risks, such as weaker guarantees, complex failure modes, or dependence on a small set of operators.

Bridges: value and risk

Bridges connect systems. They allow assets or messages to move between chains or layers. Bridges can be useful because the crypto ecosystem is fragmented. Different networks have different strengths, communities, and applications. Bridges try to reduce this fragmentation.

Bridges also add risk because they sit between security domains. They must correctly track what happened on one system and represent it on another. If bridge logic fails, funds can be misrepresented or stolen. Even when bridge code is correct, operational complexity can create vulnerabilities. As a user, treat bridges as higher-risk infrastructure compared to simple on-chain transfers. Use them with care. Prefer clear documentation, strong security practices, and conservative exposure.

Wallet UX: the adoption bottleneck

Many people think the main crypto bottleneck is blockchain speed. In practice, wallet experience is often a bigger barrier. Wallets are where users manage keys, permissions, and networks. If the wallet experience is confusing, users make costly mistakes. If the wallet experience hides risk, users approve dangerous actions. If the wallet experience is too complex, users choose custodial platforms and accept platform risk.

Good wallet UX reduces cognitive load. It makes network choice clear. It makes permissions understandable. It warns users about common scams. It also supports safe backup and recovery habits. A network can be technically advanced, but if users cannot operate it safely, adoption will remain limited.

Checklist: scale without breaking trust

1. Capacity must increase without making verification impossible for normal participants.
2. Failure modes must be clear, not hidden behind marketing.
3. Users must understand where final settlement happens and what guarantees exist.
4. Dependencies, such as bridges and oracles, must be treated as risk layers.
5. Wallet interfaces must reduce mistakes, not just add features.

Quick Check

Can you explain congestion as "demand exceeds capacity."
Can you explain Layer 1 as "the base trust layer" and Layer 2 as "a scaling layer."
Can you explain why bridges are useful and why they are risky.
Can you explain why wallet experience is a major adoption barrier.
Can you name two things a scaling solution must protect: verification and clear guarantees.

Part 3 — Markets, Trading, and Investing (Without the Hype)

Part Introduction: control risk, don't chase noise

Crypto markets are not only about technology. They are also about people. People bring fear, hope, impatience, and herd behavior. That human layer can dominate price movement, even when the underlying technology has not changed. This part helps you understand how markets actually move, so you can avoid common traps and reduce emotional decisions.

You will learn four forces that shape price action: liquidity, sentiment, narratives, and time. Liquidity is how easily an asset can be bought or sold without pushing price too much. Sentiment is the crowd's mood. Narratives are the stories people believe and repeat. Time is the cycle that repeats when many people behave in similar ways. When these forces combine, you see volatility. Volatility is not always a sign that something is wrong. It is often a sign that the market is thin, emotional, and highly reactive.

This part also separates three roles that are often mixed: trading, investing, and using. A trader needs short-term execution and strict risk control. An investor needs a longer horizon and a stronger evaluation process. A user needs safety, reliability, and utility. If you mix these roles, you can make decisions that do not match your goals.

Finally, you will get a practical framework to evaluate projects. Many projects make big claims. Your job is to verify. You will learn how to check the team, the product, real users, and traction without relying on marketing. You will also learn tokenomics in plain English, and how to spot red flags early. The purpose is not to make you confident. The purpose is to make you disciplined.

Chapter 7 — How Crypto Markets Actually Move

Opening

A person opens a price chart and feels it tells the whole truth. The chart goes up, and they assume a project is strong. The chart goes down, and they assume the project is dead. That reaction is natural, but it is incomplete. Markets do not move only because of "value." Markets move because of flows, attention, and the rules of trading. In crypto, these forces can be stronger because the market can be thinner, global, and always active. This chapter explains what actually pushes prices, why cycles repeat, why volatility is normal, and how to separate signals from noise.

Definition: what "market movement" means

Market movement is the result of buyers and sellers interacting through liquidity. Liquidity is the ease of trading without large price change. When liquidity is deep, large orders can be absorbed. When liquidity is thin, small orders can move price sharply. Crypto can have pockets of deep liquidity and pockets of thin liquidity, depending on the asset, the exchange, the time, and market interest. This is why the same news can create small movement in one asset and big movement in another.

Liquidity, sentiment, and narratives

Liquidity is not only "volume." Volume is how much trades happen. Liquidity is how much the market can handle at stable prices. You can have high volume and still have thin liquidity if trading is concentrated or if order books are shallow. Order books show current buy and sell interest. Shallow books can lead to quick price swings.

Sentiment is the crowd's emotional posture. It can be optimistic, fearful, or bored. Sentiment changes faster than fundamentals. Crypto is exposed to fast sentiment shifts because information travels quickly and is amplified by social media. A rumor can move price before truth arrives. A single influential voice can change mood for a short time. This does not mean the market is "fake." It means attention matters.

Narratives are stories that organize attention. A narrative can be "this chain is the future of finance" or "this token powers the next big app." Narratives reduce complexity into a simple sentence. That is why they spread. Narratives can be partially true, but they can also be misleading. A narrative can stay alive even when the product is weak, because people trade the story rather than the system. You should not ignore narratives. You should understand their power and limit their control over your decisions.

Market cycles and human behavior

Crypto markets often move in cycles because humans repeat behaviors. People chase momentum when prices rise. People panic when prices fall. People become confident near peaks. People become hopeless near bottoms. This is not unique to crypto. Crypto can make it more intense because volatility is high and the market runs 24/7.

A cycle often includes a build-up phase where interest grows quietly. Then comes a phase of rapid attention and rising prices. Then comes a phase of overconfidence, where risk is ignored. After that, the market can correct sharply. Corrections can be triggered by many factors, including leverage unwinding, bad news, regulation announcements, or simple exhaustion of buyers. In the final phase, many people leave, and activity cools. Then the cycle can restart when conditions change and new narratives appear.

This cycle does not guarantee profit. It explains why emotions can be predictable. The best advantage is not predicting the exact top or bottom.

The advantage is reducing emotional decisions. You can do that by using clear rules and by understanding that markets often exaggerate both optimism and fear.

Volatility: real causes

Volatility is how much price moves over time. In crypto, volatility can be high for several reasons. One reason is market structure. Some assets have limited liquidity, so trades move price more. Another reason is global 24/7 trading, which reduces "rest periods" and can amplify reactions. Another reason is concentrated ownership in some assets, which can increase sudden moves when large holders act. Another reason is leverage. Leverage means borrowed exposure. When leverage is high, forced liquidations can accelerate drops or spikes. Another reason is information quality. Crypto information can include rumors, incomplete data, and marketing, which can create fast mood shifts.

Volatility is not always a sign of bad technology. It is often a sign of a young and reactive market. Yet volatility has real consequences. It can harm users who need stable value. It can damage businesses that want predictable costs. It can increase emotional mistakes. This is why learning volatility is not a trading skill only. It is a safety skill.

Signals vs noise

A signal is information that helps you understand a system. Noise is information that distracts you without improving understanding. In crypto, noise is everywhere. Price predictions are noise unless they are backed by clear assumptions and verifiable data. Viral claims are noise unless they can be verified through credible sources. Most "urgent" posts are noise because urgency is a tactic, not evidence.

Signals tend to have three qualities. They are specific. They are verifiable. They are connected to how the system works. For example, a change in protocol rules is a signal. A documented security incident is a signal. A clear shift in regulation in a major jurisdiction can be a signal. A real increase in user activity might be a signal, but it must be measured carefully, because data can be misleading. You do not need perfect data. You need disciplined questions.

A practical method is to ask: what changed in the system. If nothing changed in technology, adoption, or regulation, then price movement may be driven mainly by flows and sentiment. That does not make it irrelevant, but it changes how you interpret it. Another method is to separate time horizons. A short-term move can be dominated by noise. Long-term outcomes are shaped by adoption, utility, and survival under regulation and security constraints.

Quick Check

Can you explain liquidity as "how easily trading happens without big price impact."
Can you explain why sentiment can move price even if technology is unchanged.
Can you name one way narratives influence behavior and decision quality.
Can you list two drivers of volatility beyond "news."
Can you describe one method to separate signal from noise.

Chapter 8 — Trading vs Investing vs Using

Opening

Many people enter crypto with one goal, but they behave like another role. They say they are "investing," but they panic-trade daily. They say they are "using," but they chase risky tokens for fast gains. The result is confusion and regret. The first step toward discipline is role clarity. This chapter explains the three roles—trader, investor, and user—and gives you a simple way to choose what fits you. It also covers risk basics and emotional mistakes, because psychology can break any strategy.

Definition: three roles, three goals

A trader tries to benefit from short-term price movement. A trader cares about timing, liquidity, spreads, and execution. An investor tries to benefit from long-term value creation. An investor cares about fundamentals, adoption, and survival. A user tries to solve a practical problem using crypto tools. A user cares about reliability, cost, safety, and legality in their context. These roles can overlap, but they should not be mixed without intention. When roles are mixed, rules become unclear, and risk control disappears.

Three roles: trader / investor / user

A trader lives in the short term. That means risk must be controlled tightly. Without strict limits, one bad move can erase many good moves. Traders also face the problem of noise. Short-term markets are driven by flows and sentiment. A trader needs a process to avoid impulsive decisions. That process can include entry rules, exit rules, and maximum loss rules.

An investor lives in a longer horizon. That means the main skill is evaluation. Evaluation is not prediction. It is assessing whether a project can survive and create real utility. Investors need patience, but they also need humility. Many projects fail. Many projects change direction. Many investors confuse popularity with durability. Investors should also separate their personal belief from evidence. Belief can motivate learning, but evidence should control allocation decisions.

A user lives in the world of daily outcomes. A user might want to send money, store value, or access a service. The user's key risks are operational. Wrong addresses, fake apps, custody failures, and compliance issues can harm users. Users should focus on safe workflows. Users should also avoid turning a tool into a bet. If the goal is payment, then stability and reliability matter more than price excitement.

Time horizon framework

Time horizon is the simplest filter for choosing your role. A short horizon means you are exposed to fast noise. A long horizon means you are exposed to long-term uncertainty. A practical way is to ask: what is your decision cycle. If you plan to act daily or weekly based on price moves, you are trading. If you plan to hold through volatility for months or years based on a thesis, you are investing. If you plan to use crypto as a rail or utility, you are using. This clarity matters because each role requires different tools and different safety rules.

Risk basics (position sizing, diversification)

Risk control begins with position sizing. Position sizing is how much of your total resources you place into one idea. You do not need complex math to respect this. The principle is simple. If one position can ruin you, it is too large. Crypto volatility makes this principle even more important. A position can go down fast. It can also become illiquid in stress. Illiquidity means you cannot exit at a fair price. This is why risk must be controlled before you enter, not after fear appears.

Diversification means not depending on one asset, one platform, or one assumption. Diversification can reduce some risks, but it does not remove market-wide risk. In many downturns, correlations rise. Correlation means assets move together. That is why diversification should be combined with other safety habits, such as avoiding excessive leverage and using secure custody practices.

This book is educational, not financial advice. Still, the concept of risk control is universal. It applies whether you trade, invest, or use. If you ignore risk, the market will teach you in a painful way.

Emotional mistakes and how to avoid them

The most common emotional mistake is chasing. Chasing means buying after a large rise because you fear missing out. Another mistake is panic selling after a sharp drop because you fear total loss. Another mistake is moving goalposts. A person says they will hold long-term, then they change the plan because of short-term noise. Another mistake is seeking confirmation. A person follows only voices that agree with their position. Another mistake is revenge trading. A person loses, then takes a bigger risk to recover quickly. These mistakes are common because they are human.

Avoiding these mistakes requires simple discipline. It requires written rules. It requires time delays before action when emotions are high. It also requires honesty about your role. If you are a user, do not chase risky assets. If you are an investor, do not treat every dip as a signal. If you are a trader, do not treat hope as a strategy.

Decision Map: what fits you?

If your main goal is learning and safety, start as a user or observer. Use small amounts, focus on security, and learn the workflows. If your main goal is long-term exposure to a thesis, act like an investor. Build an evaluation process and accept uncertainty. If your main goal is short-term opportunities and you can follow strict rules, you may choose trading, but only if you accept that most people struggle without discipline.

A practical choice is to pick one primary role for six months. This reduces confusion. It also makes learning faster, because your actions match your goals. You can adjust later as your knowledge grows.

Quick Check

Can you explain the difference between trading and investing in one paragraph.
Can you explain why a user should prioritize safety over excitement.
Can you define position sizing as "how much you risk per idea."
Can you explain why diversification helps but does not remove market-wide risk.
Can you name two emotional mistakes and one method to reduce them.

Chapter 9 — Project Evaluation Framework (The Reality Scorecard)

Opening

Many crypto projects sound impressive in a few sentences. They promise speed, community, and a future where everything changes. Marketing can be smooth, and social proof can be loud. Your job is to slow down and verify. A strong project can still be a bad investment for you. A weak project can still have a strong narrative for a while. This chapter gives you a calm framework to evaluate projects based on reality, not on noise. It focuses on team, product, real users, traction, token design, red flags, and verification habits.

Definition: evaluation as a discipline

Evaluation means checking whether claims match evidence. It does not mean predicting price. A good evaluation reduces the chance you are fooled by slogans. It also helps you compare projects fairly. The goal is not perfection. The goal is clarity. A clear "I don't know" is better than a confident guess.

Team, product, users, traction

The team matters because execution matters. A strong idea without execution can fail. A strong team with weak incentives can also fail. You should look for evidence of competence, not just titles. Evidence can include prior shipped products, clear technical documentation, and honest communication in difficult moments. Unknown information should stay unknown. If you cannot verify the team, treat that as risk.

The product matters because utility matters. Ask what the product actually does. Ask who uses it and why. Ask whether it solves a real problem or only creates a token to trade. A useful product can still fail if it is hard to use, expensive, or blocked by regulation. That is why you check the user experience and the compliance posture.

Users and traction are about real adoption, not noise. Traction means evidence of usage that is not only marketing. It might include active addresses, transaction counts, or revenue in some models, but data can be misleading. A project can inflate metrics. A project can also have real use that is not captured by public numbers. The correct stance is cautious. Look for multiple signs, not one single metric. Also look for how the project behaves during stress. Does it communicate clearly. Does it handle incidents responsibly. Does it blame users, or does it fix problems.

Tokenomics in plain English

Tokenomics is how a token's supply, demand, and incentives are designed. It answers simple questions. How many tokens exist now. Can more be created. Who holds them. When do locked tokens unlock. What does the token do inside the product. Is it needed for fees, governance, access, or rewards. Incentives matter because incentives shape behavior. If a token rewards early holders heavily while late users provide the liquidity, the system can become unstable. If a token's value depends mainly on continuous new buyers, it resembles a fragile structure. The honest evaluation asks: is there real utility and sustainable demand, or is the token mainly a marketing engine.

A key point is that tokenomics is not only about supply charts. It is about control. Who can change rules. Who can pause transfers. Who can upgrade contracts. Who holds admin keys. A token can appear decentralized but still have centralized control points. Control is not always bad. Control can allow emergency fixes. Control can also create abuse risk. You must see it clearly.

Red flags checklist

A red flag is not proof of failure. It is a reason to slow down. One red flag is unclear claims that cannot be verified. Another red flag is aggressive urgency, like "buy now or miss forever." Another red flag is hiding critical details behind vague language. Another red flag is complicated token mechanics that most users cannot explain. Another red flag is weak security practices or ignoring past incidents. Another red flag is a team that attacks critics instead of answering questions. Another red flag is dependence on one partner, one bridge, or one oracle with no backup plan.

How to verify claims

Verification is a habit, not a one-time task. Start with primary sources when possible. Primary sources include official documentation, audited code reports when available, and clear disclosures. Secondary sources include reputable research reports and serious analyses, but even these can be biased or outdated. Social media posts are the weakest form of evidence, even when they are popular.

A simple verification method is to ask: what would I need to see to believe this claim. If the claim is "we have many users," look for evidence beyond follower counts. If the claim is "we are secure," look for security practices, audits, incident history, and how risk is handled. If the claim is "we are decentralized," look for governance reality and control points. If you cannot verify, label it as unknown and treat it as risk.

Template: project scorecard

Project Name:
Problem: What real problem is being solved:
User: Who uses it, and why:
Product: What the system actually does in one paragraph:
Evidence of traction: What is verifiable, and what is unknown:
Security posture: Audits, incident history, key risks:

Control and governance: Who can change rules, and how:
Token role: What the token is for, in plain English:
Supply and unlocks: What is known, and what is unknown:
Dependencies: Key external risks, such as bridges or oracles:
Red flags: List the main concerns:
Overall clarity rating: Clear / Mixed / Unclear:
Decision status: Observe / Small test use / Avoid for now:

Quick Check

Can you explain why evaluation is different from prediction.
Can you name three areas to check: team, product, and real users.
Can you explain tokenomics as "rules that shape incentives and control."
Can you list two red flags that should make you slow down.
Can you write one project claim and describe how you would verify it.

Part 4 — Regulation, Legal Reality, and Compliance

Part Introduction: what's allowed shapes what survives

Crypto can feel borderless, but rules are not borderless. Laws are local, and enforcement is local. That reality shapes what products can exist and what businesses can offer. It also shapes what users can safely do. Many crypto failures are not only technical failures. They are compliance failures. A product may work, but it may not be allowed. A service may be popular, but it may not survive the rules in key markets.

This part gives you a calm, practical view. It does not try to turn you into a lawyer. It gives you the minimum framework to avoid dangerous assumptions. You will learn why regulators care, what KYC and AML mean in plain English, and why stablecoins receive extra attention. You will also learn how regulation differs by region at a high level, without pretending one rule fits all countries.

Then you will learn practical compliance habits. You will learn what record-keeping means and why it matters. You will learn common mistakes people make when they ignore reporting basics. This is educational only. It is not legal or tax advice. If you plan to act in the real world, you should check rules in your country and use professional help when needed.

Chapter 10 — Regulation and Legal Challenges (Global View)

Opening

A crypto product can be brilliant and still fail, because rules can stop it. A user can be careful with keys and still face trouble, because a service can freeze, close, or change access. Regulation is not a side story. It is part of the engine of adoption. If you ignore it, you misunderstand the market. If you fear it too much, you miss the real purpose. This chapter explains why regulators care, what compliance terms mean, why stablecoins get special focus, and how rules change behavior for users and firms.

Definition: what regulation means in crypto

Regulation is the set of rules that governments and authorities use to control financial activity, protect consumers, and reduce crime. In crypto, regulation often focuses on how value moves, how identities are verified, and how risks are disclosed. It can also focus on market integrity, meaning fair trading and honest information. Regulation is not one document. It is a system of laws, guidance, enforcement, and court decisions. This is why it changes over time and differs across countries.

Why regulators care

Regulators care because crypto touches money and financial stability. Money systems influence crime prevention, tax collection, and consumer protection. When value moves fast across borders, authorities worry about misuse. They also worry about fraud and scams that harm citizens. They worry about market manipulation in thin markets. They worry about companies offering financial-like products without clear safeguards. They also worry about payment systems that could affect monetary policy, especially when stablecoins and large platforms grow.

Regulators also care about transparency and accountability. In traditional finance, regulated firms must follow rules on disclosures, audits, and reporting. Many crypto products started outside those frameworks. That created innovation. It also created harm. The regulation story is often an attempt to bring similar expectations into a new domain. The result can feel messy, because crypto is both software and finance. Different agencies may treat it differently.

KYC/AML and compliance basics

KYC means "Know Your Customer." It refers to identity checks that help a company confirm who is using a service. AML means "Anti-Money Laundering." It refers to processes that aim to detect and prevent illegal use of financial systems. These processes can include monitoring transactions, reporting suspicious activity, and limiting access when risk is high. The goal is to reduce fraud, laundering, and financing of illegal activity. The methods vary by country and by service type.

In practice, KYC and AML shape the difference between a protocol and a company. A public blockchain protocol may be open. A centralized exchange is a company. The company may be required to identify users and report certain patterns. This is why user experience differs across services. Some services require identity checks before you can trade or withdraw. Some services may limit features in certain regions. Some services may request extra documentation when activity looks unusual. These actions can be frustrating, but they are often linked to legal obligations.

Stablecoins: why they get extra attention

A stablecoin is a crypto token designed to keep a stable price, often linked to a national currency. Stablecoins get extra attention because they behave like money-like instruments. They can be used for payments, trading, and savings behavior. They can also create large-scale exposure if many people rely on them for stability. Regulators often focus on stablecoins for three reasons. The first reason is reserves and backing. People want to know what supports the stable value. The second reason is redemption and liquidity. People want to know whether they can exit smoothly in stress. The third reason is systemic risk. If a stablecoin becomes widely used, its failure could harm many users and affect markets.

Stablecoins also raise questions about who is responsible. Some stablecoins are issued by companies with clear governance. Others are designed as protocols with complex mechanisms. The risk profile depends on design. The safest mindset is not to assume "stable" means "safe." Stable refers to target price behavior. Safety depends on governance, reserves, controls, and legal structure, which can vary and can be hard to verify fully without trusted information.

Regional differences (high-level)

Regulation differs by region because financial systems differ by region. Some jurisdictions treat crypto mainly as a financial asset and regulate trading platforms heavily. Some focus on payment use cases. Some focus on consumer warnings and licensing rules. Some restrict certain products, such as leveraged trading, because it can amplify harm. Some prioritize innovation and create sandbox programs. Some impose strict marketing rules to reduce misleading promotions. Many countries also treat tax reporting differently, based on local tax law and how crypto is classified.

You should avoid one dangerous assumption. Do not assume that a rule in one major market automatically applies everywhere. Also do not assume that "no one enforces it" means "it is safe." Enforcement can change. Interpretation can change. A service can also choose to restrict users from certain regions to reduce its own legal risk. That is why "regional differences" matters even if you never leave your country. Your access can still change because service providers operate globally.

What regulation changes for users and firms

For users, regulation changes onboarding, access, and privacy expectations. You may be asked to verify identity. You may be limited in what products you can use. You may face reporting obligations. You may need stronger record-keeping habits. You may also benefit from better consumer protections in regulated environments, but that depends on the jurisdiction.

For firms, regulation changes business models and costs. Companies may need licenses, compliance teams, audits, and strict controls. They may need to restrict features in some markets. They may face penalties if they fail. This can slow down growth, but it can also increase trust. A compliance-first firm may survive longer than a fast-moving firm that ignores rules. This is why regulation often shapes "what survives," not only "what is allowed today."

Real example: a user meets compliance reality

A user opens an exchange account and buys a small amount of crypto. Everything feels simple. Later, the user tries to withdraw a larger amount. The exchange asks for additional documents. The user is surprised and angry. The exchange may be reacting to internal risk rules or legal obligations. The user's mistake was assuming the first experience defines the whole system. Compliance is often layered. It can become stricter when amounts rise or patterns look unusual. The lesson is not "avoid regulated platforms." The lesson is "expect checks, keep documents ready, and avoid behavior that looks suspicious even if you are honest."

Common mistakes

A common mistake is assuming crypto is outside law because it is software. Another mistake is assuming a stablecoin is automatically safe because it is stable. Another mistake is ignoring terms of service and region restrictions, then being surprised by frozen access. Another mistake is using informal sources for legal claims, then acting on misinformation. Another mistake is confusing privacy with secrecy and taking risky steps that create bigger problems later. A final mistake is assuming compliance is only a company problem. In many countries, users also have obligations.

Quick Check

Can you explain why regulators care without using price as the main reason.
Can you define KYC and AML in plain English.
Can you explain why stablecoins get extra attention.
Can you explain why rules differ by region at a high level.
Can you name one way regulation changes life for users and one way it changes life for firms.

Chapter 11 — Taxes, Reporting, and Practical Compliance

Opening

Most people do not get into crypto because they enjoy paperwork. They enter because they want speed, access, or curiosity. Then reality arrives. Records matter. Reporting matters. Even if you never trade actively, you may still create taxable or reportable events, depending on your country. This chapter does not give tax advice. It gives a practical system mindset. It explains why record-keeping matters, what to track, how to keep it simple, and what mistakes people repeat when they avoid the basics.

Definition: what "taxes and reporting" means here

Taxes are legal obligations to pay amounts based on rules in your jurisdiction. Reporting is the obligation to disclose certain information to authorities or to regulated firms. In crypto, reporting can relate to gains, income-like receipts, business activity, or large transfers. The exact rules vary widely. Some countries treat crypto as property. Some treat it as a financial asset. Some treat certain activities as income. Some have specific reporting thresholds. Because of this variation, the safest approach is to build records first and decide the legal treatment with proper guidance later.

Why it matters

It matters because missing records can turn a small mistake into a large problem. Without records, you cannot prove cost basis. Cost basis is the original cost that helps calculate gains or losses. Without records, you may not know whether a transfer was a simple move between your wallets or a taxable disposal in your jurisdiction. Without records, you may not be able to answer basic questions from a bank, an exchange, or an accountant. Good records also reduce stress. They let you act calmly instead of guessing later.

It also matters because compliance is not only about paying. It is also about demonstrating honesty and clarity. Many problems come from confusion, not from intent. A simple log can protect you from confusion.

How it works at a high level

Most tax systems care about events. An event is an action that changes ownership, value, or entitlement. In crypto, common event types include buying, selling, swapping one asset for another, receiving rewards, receiving payments, and spending crypto on goods or services. Even if you never convert to cash, some jurisdictions still treat swaps as disposal events. This is why "I did not cash out" is not always a shield. It depends on the rules.

Reporting often focuses on traceability. Authorities want to understand flows and ownership links when needed. Regulated companies often collect identity information and transaction information. You may receive forms or summaries from platforms. These can help, but they can also be incomplete if you used multiple platforms or self-custody wallets. That is why your own record system matters.

Record-keeping simple system

A good record system is boring, consistent, and easy to maintain. You do not need complex tools to start. You need a reliable habit and a stable format.

1. Capture the "five facts" for every action.
   Date and time.
   Asset and amount.
   Platform or wallet used.

Type of action, such as buy, sell, swap, receive, send, or fee.
Reference detail, such as transaction ID or order ID.

2. Add the "why" in one short sentence.
   This helps future you understand intent.
   It also helps separate personal transfer from payment.

3. Store proof in one folder.
   Keep screenshots of trade confirmations.
   Keep CSV exports from exchanges when available.
   Keep wallet transaction links or IDs.
   Keep receipts for fiat deposits and withdrawals.

4. Reconcile monthly.
   Monthly means you review your list and fix missing details.
   This prevents year-end panic.

You can keep this in a spreadsheet, a document, or a secure note system. The tool matters less than consistency. If you use a spreadsheet, use one row per action. If you use a document, use one entry per action with the same fields every time.

Real example: the "simple swap" that becomes a headache

A user buys one asset on an exchange and later swaps it into another asset. The user thinks it is only a move inside crypto, so it is not important. Months later, the user wants to calculate gains for reporting, or a bank asks about source of funds. The user cannot remember the swap details. The user also cannot show the original cost of the first asset. The platform's history is partial because the user used more than one exchange. The result is confusion, stress, and sometimes overpayment or underreporting. A simple record at the time would have prevented this. The lesson is not fear. The lesson is discipline.

Common mistakes

A common mistake is mixing personal transfers with payments without labeling them. Another mistake is losing transaction IDs and relying on memory. Another mistake is assuming the exchange will keep perfect records forever. Another mistake is ignoring fees, even though fees can affect net outcomes. Another mistake is using multiple wallets and platforms with no consolidated log. Another mistake is downloading reports once, then never reconciling, which allows errors to build. A final mistake is taking online tax claims as universal truth. Rules differ, and advice can be wrong or outdated.

Quick Check

Can you explain why record-keeping matters even if you are not trading daily.
Can you name three "event types" that might matter for reporting in many systems.
Can you list the "five facts" you should capture for every action.
Can you explain what cost basis means in one sentence.
Can you name one mistake you will avoid by reconciling monthly.

Part 5 — Security, Scams, and Consumer Protection

Part Introduction: safety is a skill

Crypto gives you more control. That control is the benefit, and it is also the risk. In traditional finance, many safety tasks are handled by institutions. In crypto, many safety tasks move to the user. This does not mean crypto is "unsafe." It means safety becomes a personal skill, like driving or using online banking. If you do not learn the skill, the system will feel hostile. If you learn the skill, the system becomes manageable.

This part focuses on real-life safety, not fear. You will learn how custody works, and why it changes your risk. You will learn simple wallet habits that prevent most losses. You will learn how phishing works and why fake apps are so effective. You will learn what exchange risk looks like and how it shows up in practice. You will also learn scams and market manipulation patterns, because many losses happen without any technical hacking. They happen through persuasion and pressure.

The goal is calm competence. You do not need to be perfect. You need a repeatable routine. You need clear rules for what you will never do. You need a short checklist that you follow every time. When safety becomes a habit, you stop relying on luck.

Chapter 12 — Security for Real People

Opening

Most crypto losses happen the same way. They happen quickly, and they happen when someone is rushed. A person clicks a link, installs an app, approves a transaction, or shares a phrase, then tries to fix it after the damage is done. Crypto is unforgiving in that moment because it is designed to settle value without central reversal. That is why "real people security" is about preventing mistakes before they happen. This chapter explains custody types, wallet habits, phishing, fake apps, and exchange risks, using plain language and practical routines.

Definition: what security means here

Security means protecting access to your assets and protecting your decision process. Access protection is about keys, devices, and accounts. Decision protection is about avoiding manipulation, urgency, and confusion. You can have a strong password and still lose funds if you approve the wrong transaction. You can avoid scams and still lose funds if your device is compromised. Security is layered, and each layer reduces a different risk.

Custodial vs non-custodial

Custodial means someone else holds the keys. This is common with exchanges and many platforms. You log in with a password, and the platform controls the wallet. Non-custodial means you hold the keys. You control access through your wallet and recovery phrase. The difference matters because it changes who can move funds and who can block funds.

Custodial systems can be easier for beginners. They can offer password recovery and support. They can also freeze accounts, limit withdrawals, or fail as businesses. Custodial risk is business risk. It includes insolvency risk, compliance risk, and operational risk. Even a reputable platform can face outages or policy changes. Non-custodial systems reduce platform dependence, but they increase personal responsibility. If you lose your recovery phrase, you may lose access permanently. If you approve malicious transactions, there may be no customer support to reverse them.

A practical mindset is to match custody type to purpose. If you are learning, you may start small on a custodial platform to reduce complexity. If you hold meaningful value long-term, you may prefer non-custodial storage, but only after you learn safe habits. Many experienced users also split risk. They keep a small "spending" amount in a hot wallet and store long-term amounts in safer setups.

Wallet safety habits

Good wallet safety is not complicated. It is consistent. The first habit is protecting your recovery phrase. The recovery phrase is the master key. Anyone who has it can often take your funds. You should never type it into random websites. You should never share it with support accounts. You should never store it in screenshots or cloud notes. A safer approach is offline storage in a place you control.

The second habit is device hygiene. Use trusted devices. Keep software updated. Avoid installing unknown extensions. Many wallet attacks happen through browser extensions and fake updates. The third habit is transaction discipline. Before you approve, you pause. You check the address. You check the amount. You check the network. You also check what the approval allows. Some approvals grant permission to spend tokens later. This can be dangerous if the contract is malicious or later compromised.

The fourth habit is separation. Use different wallets for different purposes. Use one wallet for long-term holding with minimal interaction. Use another wallet for experimentation. This reduces the chance that a risky click drains your main holdings. The fifth habit is small tests. When you use a new address or service, send a small amount first. Confirm it arrived. Then proceed. This is not paranoia. It is good operational practice.

Phishing and fake apps

Phishing is an attempt to trick you into giving up access or approving a harmful action. It often looks official. It uses logos, urgent language, and fake support messages. It can come by email, messaging apps, social media, or search ads. Phishing works because it creates pressure. Pressure reduces thinking.

Fake apps are a related threat. A fake wallet app may look like a real wallet. A fake exchange app may look normal. The goal is to capture your credentials or recovery phrase, or to route approvals through malicious paths. The safest defense is to avoid searching random links. Use official sources and verified app stores where possible. Even then, stay cautious. Fake apps can still appear. The second defense is to treat your recovery phrase as untouchable. If any app asks for it unexpectedly, that is a danger signal.

Another common technique is fake "airdrop" or "bonus" claims. A site asks you to connect your wallet and approve a transaction to receive something. The transaction actually grants permission to drain assets. This is why you must read approval prompts carefully. If the prompt is confusing, stop. Confusion is a reason to pause, not a reason to click.

Exchange risk

An exchange is a company. Companies have risks. The first risk is custody risk. If the exchange holds your assets, you are exposed to its security and solvency. The second risk is operational risk. Exchanges can go down during high volatility. Withdrawals can be delayed. Trading can be paused. The third risk is compliance risk. An exchange can restrict accounts due to legal obligations or policy changes. The fourth risk is account risk. Attackers often target exchange accounts because they can bypass on-chain security by stealing login access.

Good exchange hygiene includes strong passwords and two-factor authentication. Two-factor authentication means a second proof, such as an app code, not a simple SMS when possible. It also includes avoiding reused passwords, avoiding logging in on public devices, and watching for phishing emails that mimic exchange alerts.

A practical rule is simple. Use exchanges as places to convert or trade, not as permanent storage for large long-term holdings. If you do keep funds on an exchange, treat it as a calculated exposure, not as a default.

One-page security checklist

Before you install any wallet or app, you confirm it is the official one.
Before you connect a wallet to any site, you verify the URL carefully.
Before you approve any transaction, you pause and read the approval details.
You never share your recovery phrase, and you never type it into websites.
You store recovery information offline in a secure way you control.
You use two-factor authentication on all custodial accounts.
You separate long-term storage from daily-use wallets.
You test with small amounts when using new addresses or services.
You keep your device and browser updated and avoid unknown extensions.
If you feel rushed, you stop and return later with a clear mind.

Quick Check

Can you explain custodial vs non-custodial in plain English.
Can you name two benefits and two risks of custodial platforms.

Can you name three wallet habits that prevent common losses.

Can you describe phishing as "pressure plus deception," and name one defense.

Can you state one rule you will follow every time you approve a transaction.

Chapter 13 — Scams, Fraud, and Market Manipulation

Opening

Many people imagine a scam as a person stealing passwords. In crypto, scams often look like opportunity. They look like early access, insider tips, exclusive groups, and fast profits. The attacker does not need to break code. The attacker only needs to shape your choices. Market manipulation is similar. It relies on emotion, not on truth. This chapter explains common patterns such as pump and dump schemes, rug pulls, fake audits, influencer traps, and practical verification steps.

Definition: scams and manipulation

A scam is a planned deception designed to take your money or access. Market manipulation is an attempt to influence price artificially for profit. Both use information control. Both use timing. Both often use social proof. In crypto, scams spread fast because global access is easy and because many users are new. The best defense is pattern recognition and slow decision-making.

Pump & dump explained

A pump and dump is a coordinated effort to push price up quickly, then sell into the rise. The "pump" phase uses hype, charts, and urgent messaging. The "dump" phase happens when insiders sell while new buyers are still entering. The new buyers become the exit liquidity. Exit liquidity means the people whose buying allows others to sell at higher prices.

These schemes often target small tokens with thin liquidity because they are easier to move. The promoters may show huge short-term gains and claim a "community movement." They may discourage questions and frame doubt as weakness. The simplest defense is to treat sudden hype as a warning, not as a signal. Another defense is to check liquidity, token distribution, and whether the project has real utility beyond price excitement.

Rug pulls and fake audits

A rug pull happens when project insiders create a system, attract funds, then remove value or abandon the project. This can happen in different ways. Liquidity can be removed from a pool. Tokens can be minted unexpectedly. Contract permissions can be abused. The project can vanish after collecting funds. Many rug pulls are not technical miracles. They are permission misuse and weak governance.

Fake audits add a layer of credibility. An audit is a review of code by a third party. Audits can help, but they are not a guarantee. A fake audit is worse because it creates false confidence. Some scams use fake logos or edited documents. Others use low-quality reviews that do not cover the real risk. A serious evaluation checks who performed the audit, what was reviewed, and whether issues were fixed. If you cannot verify the audit, treat it as unknown.

Influencer hype traps

Influencers can shape attention. Some are honest. Some are paid. Some are careless. The trap is not only malicious intent. The trap is that incentives differ. An influencer may earn from referrals, token allocations, or content engagement. That incentive can tilt the message toward excitement. The audience experiences the message as advice, even if it is presented as entertainment.

A common pattern is the "limited time" message. Another pattern is the "this is not financial advice" sentence followed by strong persuasion. Another pattern is selective evidence, such as showing winners but never showing losses. The defense is to shift from personality trust to evidence checks. You can respect someone's communication skill while still refusing to outsource your decisions.

Verification steps

Verification is your shield. You do not need deep technical skill to verify basic claims. You need a routine. You check what is actually built. You check who controls critical permissions. You check whether the project explains risk clearly. You check whether documentation is coherent and consistent. You check whether the team is transparent in a way you can verify. You check whether the token has a clear role beyond price. You check whether the project depends on fragile mechanisms.

When you cannot verify, you label it unknown. Unknown is not a judgment. Unknown is a risk category. Many people get harmed because they treat unknown as "probably fine." In crypto, "probably fine" is not a safety standard.

Scam spotting drill

Imagine you see a new token trending. The message says the token will "change everything" and the price is rising fast. You are invited to a group that promises early access. The group tells you to connect your wallet to claim a bonus. You feel pressure because others are posting profits. You stop and apply the drill.

You ask: what problem is solved, and who uses it. You ask: is there a real product, or only a token. You ask: who controls the contract, and can they change supply or permissions. You ask: what is the source of this link, and is it official. You ask: what happens if I do nothing today. If the answer is "I miss a hype event," that is not a serious loss. You also ask: what is the worst-case outcome if this is a scam. If the worst case is losing access to your wallet, then the correct action is to stop.

This drill works because it reintroduces time. Scams hate time. Scams need urgency. When you slow down, the scam loses power.

Quick Check

Can you explain a pump and dump as "hype up, sell into buyers."
Can you explain a rug pull as "insiders remove value or abuse permissions."
Can you explain why an audit can help but cannot guarantee safety.
Can you name two influencer traps and one defense method.
Can you describe the scam spotting drill in your own words, in one paragraph.

Part 6 — Real Applications and Industry Use Cases

Part Introduction: where crypto becomes useful

In the earlier parts, you learned what crypto is, how markets behave, and why rules and safety matter. In this part, you move from "ideas" to "use." Use is where the technology either earns trust or loses it. Many debates about crypto become clearer when you ask one simple question. What job is this system doing that older systems struggle to do. When crypto solves a real job, it can create value even without hype. When crypto does not solve a job, it often becomes a story that fades.

This part focuses on five use areas. Payments and remittances show crypto as a money rail. DeFi shows crypto as a set of financial tools built from code. NFTs show crypto as a system for digital ownership and membership. Tokenization shows crypto as a way to represent real-world assets with digital records. Enterprise and government use cases show crypto as infrastructure for auditing, identity, and coordination.

You will also see a pattern. Every useful use case has a limit. Payments face compliance and user protection. DeFi faces smart contract risk and complex failure modes. NFTs face weak quality control and hype cycles. Tokenization faces legal reality and data truth issues. Enterprise projects face organizational friction and unclear incentives. The goal is not to accept or reject crypto as a whole. The goal is to understand where it fits, where it does not, and how to evaluate each case with calm discipline.

Chapter 14 — Payments and Remittances

Opening

Most people do not wake up wanting "blockchain." They want money to arrive quickly, safely, and with fair cost. Payments and remittances are the simplest place to judge crypto, because the goal is clear. Move value from one person to another. Yet the real world adds friction. Banks can be slow across borders. Fees can be hard to predict. Compliance checks can delay transfers. Crypto can help in some situations, but it can also add new risks. This chapter explains when crypto helps, why stablecoins matter, how to handle volatility, and how a small business could use a disciplined workflow.

Definition: payments and remittances in plain English

Payments are value transfers for goods and services. Remittances are cross-border transfers, often person to person, often for family support. The key pain points are speed, cost, reliability, access, and transparency of fees. Traditional systems can work well in many places. They can also fail in high-friction corridors, where banks are limited, fees are high, and settlement is slow.

When crypto helps

Crypto can help when it reduces friction in a specific link of the chain. It can help when a sender lacks access to fast international banking. It can help when recipients need value quickly, and local options are limited. It can help when the sender and recipient can both access reliable on-ramps and off-ramps. On-ramp means converting local money into crypto. Off-ramp means converting crypto into local money.

Crypto can also help with transparency. A user can often track an on-chain transfer. That does not solve every problem, but it can reduce uncertainty about whether the transfer was sent. It can also help in business payments when a merchant wants a faster settlement workflow, or when a business wants to pay global contractors in a consistent way. These benefits are real, but they depend on the surrounding services, not only on the blockchain.

Crypto does not help when the weakest link is the off-ramp. If the recipient cannot easily convert to what they need, the transfer is not useful. Crypto also does not help when the legal environment makes use unsafe. It does not help when the user cannot manage wallet security. It does not help when fees and congestion make transfers expensive at peak times.

Stablecoins for payments

Stablecoins are often used for payments because they aim to reduce price movement. Price movement is the main pain point when you want to use a volatile asset as money. A stablecoin can feel closer to digital cash behavior. It can make budgeting easier. It can reduce the risk that a payment loses value before it is spent.

Still, stablecoins are not all the same. The design and governance matter. Some rely on reserves and issuers. Some rely on mechanisms that may be complex. The stable label describes a target, not a guarantee. For payment use, the practical question is whether the stablecoin is widely accepted, easy to redeem, and supported by reliable services in your region. If those conditions are not met, it can create new friction.

Volatility handling

If you use a volatile asset for payment, you must manage time and exposure. The simplest method is to reduce holding time. Convert close to the payment time. Transfer quickly. Convert back if needed. The longer you hold, the more you are exposed to price swings.

A second method is to use stablecoins for the transfer leg. This can reduce exposure during the travel time. A third method is to split amounts. A small test transfer can confirm the address and network. Then the main transfer follows. This reduces operational risk, not market risk, but it matters.

Volatility handling also includes fee awareness. Some networks have variable fees. Fee spikes can act like a hidden volatility cost. If fees surge, the effective cost of sending rises. A disciplined workflow checks fees before sending, especially during market stress.

Mini Case: small business workflow

Imagine a small design studio that pays a contractor in another country each month. Bank transfers are slow and fees are unclear. The studio wants a predictable, repeatable method. The studio decides to use a stablecoin transfer, but it sets strict rules.

The studio uses a dedicated business wallet for transfers only. It stores recovery information offline and limits device use. It selects one reputable on-ramp that supports its region. It also selects one off-ramp the contractor can use reliably. The studio pays only after a test transfer confirms the contractor's address. The studio records every step with date, amount, network, fee, and transaction ID. It also keeps screenshots of conversions and receipts. The studio sets a monthly routine, so transfers are not rushed. It avoids sending during known market panic periods, when congestion is high.

Over time, the studio gets a workflow that is faster than its bank alternative. It also gains transparency in fees and settlement timing. Yet the studio still faces limits. Sometimes the off-ramp delays withdrawals. Sometimes the platform asks for compliance checks. Sometimes fees spike. The studio can tolerate these issues because it built slack and documentation. The lesson is simple. Payments can be improved with crypto, but only when the workflow is designed like a business process, not like a gamble.

Common mistakes

A common mistake is sending to the wrong network or wrong address. Another mistake is skipping a test transfer for a new recipient. Another mistake is holding volatile assets too long before payment. Another mistake is assuming a stablecoin is risk-free. Another mistake is ignoring compliance requirements until a transfer is blocked. Another mistake is failing to keep records, then being unable to explain flows later.

Quick Check

Can you explain when crypto helps in payments in one paragraph.
Can you explain why stablecoins are often used for transfers.
Can you describe one method to reduce volatility exposure.
Can you explain why the off-ramp is often the real bottleneck.
Can you describe one safety rule a business should follow every time.

Chapter 15 — DeFi Without Buzzwords

Opening

DeFi is often described with big words and fast promises. That style creates confusion and bad decisions. DeFi becomes clearer when you treat it like a set of basic financial functions built with code. These functions include trading, lending, borrowing, and earning yield. The difference is not the function. The difference is the structure. DeFi often uses smart contracts instead of a central operator. That structure can reduce some costs and open access. It also introduces new technical and operational risks. This chapter explains what DeFi is, maps the main components, explains key risks, and shows when avoiding DeFi can be the best decision.

Definition: what DeFi really is

DeFi means decentralized finance. In practice, it usually means financial services built on public blockchains using smart contracts. Users interact with code through wallets. There may be no single company holding user funds in the same way a bank does. Yet DeFi still depends on developers, interfaces, governance, and data feeds. So "decentralized" is not a magic shield. It is a design goal with degrees.

What DeFi is trying to do is simple. It tries to provide financial functions with fewer middle layers. It tries to use transparent rules and automated execution. It also tries to allow composability. Composability means one protocol can connect to another like building blocks. This can speed innovation. It can also spread risk across systems.

DEX, lending, liquidity (simple map)

A DEX is a decentralized exchange. It allows users to trade tokens through smart contract rules rather than a central order book controlled by one company. Many DEX designs use liquidity pools. A liquidity pool is a pool of tokens provided by users. Liquidity providers earn fees when trades pass through the pool. This system can work, but it creates new risks and new math. It also means prices are influenced by pool design and arbitrage.

Lending protocols allow users to supply assets and earn interest-like returns, while others borrow by posting collateral. Collateral is an asset locked to secure a loan. Many DeFi loans are over-collateralized, meaning borrowers must lock more value than they borrow. This reduces default risk but increases liquidation risk. Liquidation is when collateral is sold if the borrower's position falls below required thresholds.

Liquidity is the heart of DeFi. Liquidity determines how easily trades happen and how stable prices are. Liquidity also attracts attention, which attracts more activity, which can attract risk. When liquidity dries up, price moves become harsher, and liquidations can cascade.

A simple mental map is this. DEX is for swapping. Lending is for borrowing and supplying. Liquidity pools are the infrastructure that lets swaps and other actions run smoothly. Oracles feed prices into lending rules. Bridges connect DeFi across networks. Each piece can fail, and failures can spread.

Main risks: smart contracts, liquidation, de-pegs

Smart contract risk is the risk that code has a bug, a weakness, or a design flaw. A contract can be exploited. A contract can also fail under rare conditions. Audits help, but they are not a guarantee. If you cannot understand the core risk, you should reduce exposure or avoid the system.

Liquidation risk is the risk that your collateral is sold automatically when price moves against you. This can happen quickly in volatile markets. It can happen even if you planned to hold long-term. Liquidation is not "unfair" in code terms. It is the rule of the system. Many users lose money because they underestimate how fast liquidation can happen, especially during spikes in volatility and congestion.

De-peg risk is a stablecoin risk. A de-peg is when a stablecoin's price breaks away from its target. This can happen because of reserve issues, market panic, liquidity problems, or design weaknesses. De-pegs can damage DeFi strategies that assume stable value. They can also trigger liquidations, because collateral values change unexpectedly.

There are also hidden risks. Interface risk matters because most users access DeFi through websites and apps. A malicious interface can trick approvals. Governance risk matters because rules can change. Oracle risk matters because wrong prices can trigger wrong outcomes. Bridge risk matters because cross-chain assets depend on bridge integrity.

When to avoid DeFi

Avoid DeFi when you cannot afford to lose what you put in. Avoid DeFi when you do not have time to learn basic safety habits. Avoid DeFi when your actions depend on stable conditions, because DeFi can become unstable during market stress. Avoid DeFi when you are attracted mainly by high returns with no clear explanation. In finance, high returns usually mean high risk, even when the risk is hidden.

Avoid DeFi when you cannot verify what the system does. If documentation is vague, or if risk is minimized, that is a warning. Avoid DeFi when you feel rushed. DeFi punishes rushed decisions because approvals can be irreversible.

Common mistakes

A common mistake is confusing "decentralized" with "safe." Another mistake is chasing yield without understanding the source. Another mistake is using leverage without understanding liquidation mechanics. Another mistake is trusting stablecoins without understanding de-peg risk. Another mistake is approving token spending permissions widely, then forgetting. Another mistake is using a single wallet for everything, which increases blast radius.

Quick Check

Can you define DeFi as "financial functions built with smart contracts."
Can you explain what a DEX is in one paragraph.
Can you explain liquidation risk in one paragraph.
Can you explain de-peg risk as "stable value breaking under stress."
Can you name one reason to avoid DeFi that is not about fear.

Chapter 16 — NFTs and Digital Ownership (Beyond Art)

Opening

NFTs became famous through art headlines and wild prices. That period distorted the public understanding. It made NFTs look like a lottery. Yet the core idea behind NFTs is not art. The core idea is unique digital ownership recorded in a way that can be verified. That can support tickets, memberships, identity-like credentials, and proof of rights. This chapter explains what NFTs are in practical terms, where they can be useful, why hype distorted the space, and what realistic future paths might look like.

Definition: what an NFT is

An NFT is a non-fungible token. Non-fungible means not interchangeable like cash. One unit is not the same as another unit. An NFT can represent a unique item or a unique right. The token exists on a blockchain. Ownership can be transferred. Metadata can point to content or define rules, depending on the design. The blockchain record helps prove ownership history, but it does not automatically prove everything about the real-world meaning. The meaning depends on the system around the NFT.

Use cases: tickets, membership, IP

Tickets are a strong use case because tickets are unique and event-based. An NFT ticket can help reduce counterfeits when designed well. It can also allow programmable rules, such as resale limits or verified transfers. Yet the event organizer still matters. If the organizer does not honor the NFT, ownership is meaningless. So the use case works best when the organizer is trusted and integrates the NFT system properly.

Membership is another use case. An NFT can act like a membership badge. It can grant access to content, communities, or services. This can reduce the need for repeated logins across platforms, but it also introduces privacy trade-offs. A public wallet can reveal membership ownership. That may be acceptable or unacceptable depending on the context.

IP and rights are a complex use case. An NFT can represent proof that a person holds a digital item, but legal rights do not automatically transfer unless the legal terms say so. Many misunderstandings came from assuming "I own the NFT" means "I own the copyright." That is often false. The correct approach is to treat the NFT as a pointer to a set of rights defined by terms. If the terms are unclear, the rights are unclear.

Why hype distorted NFTs

Hype distorted NFTs because price became the story. Many projects focused on scarcity marketing rather than real utility. People bought because others bought. That behavior fueled bubbles. Some buyers thought they were buying long-term cultural assets. Others thought they were flipping for profit. Many projects delivered little beyond images and promises.

Another distortion came from weak consumer understanding. Many users did not know what they were actually owning. The token might point to a file stored on a server that could change or disappear. The project might control the metadata. The community might rely on a platform that could shut down. These details matter because ownership without durability is fragile.

Practical future paths

A realistic future path is "NFTs as a primitive," not "NFTs as a mania." The primitive is unique digital identity and ownership. We may see NFTs used quietly in loyalty systems, gaming assets, tickets, and digital credentials. We may see better standards for metadata durability and rights clarity. We may see more regulation around marketing claims and consumer protection, which can reduce fraud.

Another practical path is integration with real services. When an NFT grants something useful, people stop caring about speculative resale. They care about access and experience. That can make the space healthier. Yet it will also reduce the "get rich" narrative, which is good for safety.

Common mistakes

A common mistake is assuming an NFT automatically grants legal rights. Another mistake is ignoring where the media is stored and how durable it is. Another mistake is buying because of social proof rather than utility. Another mistake is connecting wallets to random mint sites and approving dangerous permissions. Another mistake is expecting liquidity in a thin market, then being unable to sell.

Quick Check

Can you define an NFT as "a unique token with verifiable ownership." Can you name two use cases beyond art and explain one in a paragraph. Can you explain why "owning the NFT" does not always mean owning the copyright. Can you name one reason hype was harmful to the NFT space. Can you describe one practical future path that is not speculation-driven.

Chapter 17 — Tokenization and Real-World Assets

Opening

Tokenization is one of the most promising and most misunderstood ideas in crypto. It sounds simple. Put a real-world asset on a blockchain. Make it easier to trade. Make ownership clearer. In practice, tokenization sits at the boundary between law, custody, and data truth. The hardest part is not the token. The hardest part is connecting the token to the real-world asset in a way that courts, regulators, and institutions accept. This chapter explains what tokenization means, the key challenges, and where it might scale first.

Definition: what tokenization means

Tokenization means representing an asset or a claim as a digital token. The token can represent ownership, a right to payment, access, or a share of something. The blockchain can provide transparency and a record of transfers. The token can also carry rules, such as transfer restrictions. Tokenization can be used for financial assets, real estate interests, commodities exposure, invoices, or other claims. The details depend on legal structure.

The key distinction is between the record and the reality. A blockchain record can show that a token moved. It does not automatically prove that the real asset moved legally, or that the token holder has enforceable rights. Enforceability depends on contracts, legal recognition, and compliance.

Legal + custody + data truth challenges

Legal challenges include classification and compliance. A token that represents a financial claim may be treated as a regulated instrument. Rules can require licensing, disclosure, investor suitability checks, and reporting. Rules vary by jurisdiction. Because rules vary, global tokenization is hard. Many systems start in controlled environments with limited participants.

Custody challenges include who holds the underlying asset and how it is protected. If a token represents a real asset, someone must custody that asset, or there must be a structure that guarantees control. Custody can be central, such as a regulated custodian, or it can be distributed in some designs. Either way, custody must be trustworthy. If custody is weak, token ownership is meaningless.

Data truth challenges are often overlooked. Tokenization requires truthful inputs. If a token claims to represent a warehouse inventory unit, then the inventory record must be accurate. If the data source lies, the token lies. If the asset is double-counted, the token system can hide fraud rather than prevent it. This is why tokenization is not only a blockchain problem. It is a governance and auditing problem. The "oracle" problem returns here, but in a real-world form.

Where it can scale first

Tokenization is more likely to scale first where three conditions exist. The asset is standardized. Ownership rules are clear. The ecosystem already uses digital systems and audits.

This can include certain financial instruments where regulation is already structured. It can include settlement systems where speed and transparency reduce costs. It can include supply chain contexts where a digital record improves coordination and reduces dispute, but only when there are strong controls on data entry and verification. It can also include limited networks, such as enterprise consortiums, where participants are known and legal agreements are strong.

Tokenization is less likely to scale quickly in messy asset classes where ownership is disputed, records are weak, and local laws are complex. It is also less likely to scale where fraud incentives are high and verification is weak. The technology cannot fix broken governance by itself.

Common mistakes

A common mistake is thinking tokenization removes legal work. It often increases legal work. Another mistake is assuming a blockchain record guarantees real-world enforcement. Another mistake is ignoring custody and assuming the token is the asset. Another mistake is trusting data feeds without strong audit controls. Another mistake is marketing tokenization as "instant liquidity" without explaining restrictions and compliance.

Quick Check

Can you define tokenization as "representing a real-world claim with a token."
Can you explain why legal enforceability is separate from on-chain transfer.
Can you name the three big challenges: legal, custody, and data truth.
Can you describe one context where tokenization may scale first.
Can you name one reason tokenization may fail even if the blockchain works.

Chapter 18 — Enterprise and Government Uses

Opening

Enterprises and governments do not adopt technology because it is exciting. They adopt because it reduces cost, reduces risk, or improves coordination. Many blockchain pilots fail because they start with the technology and search for a problem. A better approach starts with the problem and tests whether blockchain is the right tool. This chapter explores enterprise and government use cases like identity, audit trails, and supply chains. It explains why pilots fail and provides a simple framework for deciding when blockchain fits.

Definition: enterprise and government use cases

Enterprise use cases focus on business processes across teams and partners. Government use cases focus on public records, identity, and services where trust and accountability matter. In both cases, the real challenge is coordination among stakeholders. Technology can support coordination. It cannot replace it.

Identity, audit trails, supply chains

Identity use cases aim to improve how people prove who they are, or what rights they have, without repeating verification everywhere. Some systems aim to give users more control over credentials. This can reduce friction and reduce data duplication. Yet identity is sensitive. Privacy and legal compliance matter. A public chain can expose patterns. A private system can centralize power. A good identity solution balances usability, privacy, and trust.

Audit trails are about record integrity. A record that cannot be easily changed can reduce disputes. It can also improve accountability. Yet audit trails are only as good as the input data. If the input is false, the immutable record becomes an immutable lie. This is why audit trail use cases need strong input controls and clear responsibility.

Supply chains involve many parties. They also involve documents, shipments, and inspections. In theory, a shared ledger can reduce reconciliation work and improve traceability. In practice, supply chains are messy. Different parties use different systems. Data formats differ. Incentives differ. Many participants do not want transparency that exposes mistakes. A blockchain can help only when incentives and governance are designed carefully, and when integration costs are justified.

Why pilots fail

Pilots often fail because of unclear ownership. No one has authority to enforce adoption across participants. Pilots also fail because the problem is not strong. If a database can solve it, blockchain adds cost without benefit. Pilots fail because governance is weak. Participants disagree about rules, access, and control. Pilots fail because data quality is poor. Pilots fail because legal and compliance teams are not involved early. Pilots fail because the system is too complex for users, so work returns to manual processes.

Pilots also fail because incentives are misaligned. One party pays the cost, another party receives the benefit. Without shared incentive, adoption stalls.

Framework: when blockchain fits

Blockchain fits better when these conditions are present.

First, there are multiple parties who do not fully trust one another. Second, they need a shared record of truth. Third, there is a clear cost in disputes or reconciliation today. Fourth, there is a clear governance model for who can write, read, and update rules. Fifth, data entry can be verified, and responsibility is clear. Sixth, the system can be integrated into real workflows with minimal friction.

If these conditions are not present, blockchain may be the wrong tool. A standard database may be faster, cheaper, and easier to maintain. Choosing the simpler tool is not a defeat. It is good engineering.

Common mistakes

A common mistake is choosing blockchain for marketing value. Another mistake is ignoring governance until late. Another mistake is treating "immutable" as automatically good. Another mistake is ignoring privacy requirements. Another mistake is underestimating integration cost with legacy systems. Another mistake is assuming that one pilot success guarantees scalable adoption.

Quick Check

Can you name two enterprise use cases and explain one in a paragraph.
Can you explain why data truth matters even with an immutable ledger.
Can you explain one reason pilots fail that is not technical.
Can you explain the "when blockchain fits" framework in your own words.
Can you name one case where a normal database is likely the better choice.

Part 7 — Challenges and Opportunities (Strategic Lens)

Part Introduction: the industry's real battlefield

Crypto is not only a technology story. It is a coordination story. It is also a trust story. The real battlefield is not "who has the smartest code." The real battlefield is whether ordinary people can use the system safely, whether businesses can adopt it without legal fear, and whether the industry can mature without repeating avoidable failures. Many debates focus on price. Price is loud, but it is not the foundation. The foundation is infrastructure, user experience, security, governance, and compliance.

In this part, you look at crypto as an industry under pressure. You identify the biggest challenges that block adoption. You also identify the strongest opportunity paths that can survive reality. The goal is strategic clarity. Strategic clarity means you can separate long-term themes from short-term noise. It also means you can evaluate products and narratives with calm discipline.

You will see a pattern. Many challenges are not "unsolved science." They are "unsolved operations." They involve better design, better incentives, and better trust systems. You will also see that many opportunities are quiet. They are not built for hype. They are built for utility, reliability, and compliance. Those are the conditions that allow survival.

Chapter 19 — The Biggest Challenges Facing Crypto

Opening

If crypto is so powerful, why is it still hard for normal people. The answer is not one problem. It is a stack of problems. Each problem amplifies the others. Poor user experience leads to mistakes. Mistakes reduce trust. Low trust increases regulation pressure. Regulation pressure pushes activity into unsafe corners. Unsafe corners create new scandals. This cycle is the real challenge. This chapter explains the biggest obstacles, including scalability, user experience, governance, security, regulatory uncertainty, and fragmentation.

Definition: "challenges" in an industry sense

A challenge is not only a technical limitation. A challenge is anything that prevents stable adoption. Stable adoption means repeated use by many people without constant fear. It means businesses can rely on the system. It means users can learn once and operate safely. In crypto, the challenges span code, design, policy, and behavior.

Scalability, UX, governance

Scalability is the ability of networks to handle many users without extreme cost or delay. When a network becomes congested, fees can rise and transfers can slow. This breaks payment use cases and frustrates users. Many scaling solutions exist, but scaling remains a challenge because it is not only throughput. It is also reliability and simplicity.

User experience is a bigger problem than most people admit. Wallets can be confusing. Addresses are long and unforgiving. Network choices can be unclear. Approvals can be risky. Users are asked to understand concepts they never needed in online banking. When the learning curve is steep, adoption slows. When onboarding is confusing, scams become more effective.

Governance is about how changes happen. In crypto, governance can be formal or informal. Formal governance may use voting systems. Informal governance may rely on developer influence and community norms. Governance becomes hard because different stakeholders want different outcomes. Users want safety and stability. Builders want speed and freedom. Businesses want predictable rules. Investors want returns. Governance is also hard because upgrades can create winners and losers. When governance is weak, disputes split communities and fragment liquidity.

Security and trust

Security is a constant challenge because crypto is valuable and often irreversible. Attackers target users, platforms, bridges, and contracts. Even if a core chain is strong, the ecosystem around it may be weak. Many losses happen through phishing and social engineering. Many losses also happen through code vulnerabilities in smart contracts. Trust is damaged when users see repeated hacks or collapses. Trust is also damaged when projects hide risk and sell dreams.

Trust is not only about honesty. It is about predictability. If users do not know what will happen in stress, they cannot trust the system. If platforms change rules abruptly, users lose confidence. If fees spike unexpectedly, users lose confidence. If a stablecoin breaks its peg, users lose confidence. These events teach people that crypto is "unstable," even when specific tools are stable. The industry must earn trust through consistent behavior, not through marketing.

Regulatory uncertainty

Regulatory uncertainty blocks investment and adoption because businesses need clear boundaries. When rules are unclear, companies cannot plan. They may avoid certain markets. They may restrict products. They may face legal action after building. Users also suffer because access can change suddenly. A service may shut down features in one region. An exchange may pause withdrawals for compliance reasons. These changes create fear and inconvenience.

Uncertainty also creates uneven competition. Some firms follow strict compliance, which costs more. Others avoid it until enforcement arrives. This can reward bad behavior in the short term. That slows maturity. Over time, stronger regulation clarity can help, but only if it is balanced. Overly strict rules can push activity into unsafe spaces. Weak rules can allow fraud to grow. This balance is difficult, and it differs by country.

Fragmentation and interoperability

Fragmentation means the ecosystem is split across many networks, wallets, standards, and platforms. Interoperability means those pieces can work together. Fragmentation creates confusion and risk. Assets move across chains through bridges. Bridges can fail. Users may hold assets on multiple networks and struggle to manage them. Developers must choose where to build, which can split communities.

Interoperability is hard because systems have different security models and different consensus rules. Connecting them can introduce weak points. A system is often only as strong as its weakest link. This is why cross-chain solutions are a major risk area. It is also why users should treat cross-chain movement with discipline.

Real example: a normal user hits the stack

A user buys a token on one network because fees are low. Later, the user wants to move it to another network to use an application. The user finds many bridge options and does not know which is safe. The bridge website looks official, but it is a clone. The user connects a wallet and approves a permission. Funds disappear. The user blames crypto as a whole. The deeper issue is the stack of challenges. Fragmentation created complexity. UX made it confusing. Security risk was high. Trust was fragile. This example shows why solving one layer alone is not enough.

Common mistakes

A common mistake is thinking scalability is only about speed, not usability. Another mistake is assuming users will learn complex workflows without support. Another mistake is treating governance as politics and ignoring it, even though it shapes outcomes. Another mistake is trusting brand names without understanding risk boundaries. Another mistake is assuming regulation is an enemy rather than a constraint that can shape survival. Another mistake is moving assets across chains impulsively without a clear purpose.

Quick Check

Can you explain why crypto challenges are a "stack," not one problem.
Can you explain how poor UX increases scam success.
Can you name two reasons governance is hard in crypto.
Can you explain why regulatory uncertainty harms both firms and users.
Can you explain why fragmentation increases risk for ordinary users.

Chapter 20 — Opportunities in the Digital Currency Market

Opening

Opportunities in crypto are real, but they are not evenly distributed. The strongest opportunities are usually not the loudest. They are built around reliability, risk control, and compliance. They also aim at real pain points, not abstract ideology. This chapter maps four opportunity lanes: stablecoins and quiet adoption, infrastructure and custody services, compliance-first products, and emerging market use cases. It also provides a one-page opportunity map you can use as a simple lens.

Definition: "opportunity" in a strategic lens

An opportunity is a repeatable value creation path that can survive reality. Reality includes security threats, regulation, and user behavior. A true opportunity does not rely on constant new buyers. It relies on utility. It also aligns incentives across users, businesses, and authorities, or at least reduces conflict.

Stablecoins and "quiet adoption"

Stablecoins are one of the most practical crypto tools because they reduce price volatility for everyday use. Quiet adoption means people use the tool without caring about the ideology. They care about speed and cost. Stablecoins can support cross-border payments, merchant settlement, and treasury operations for businesses that operate globally. They can also reduce friction in regions where banking is slow or expensive.

The opportunity is not only the stablecoin itself. The opportunity is the system around it. The system includes compliant issuance, transparent reserves, secure custody, reliable on-ramps, and good user interfaces. Stablecoins can also support new forms of business-to-business settlement. They can reduce settlement time and provide clearer audit trails. These benefits are practical, but they depend on regulation and trust.

Infrastructure and custody services

As crypto matures, infrastructure becomes more important than speculation. Infrastructure includes wallets, security layers, identity tools, compliance tooling, data services, and reliable settlement rails. Custody services are especially important for institutions that cannot hold keys casually. Institutional custody requires controls, approvals, auditing, and insurance-like risk frameworks, though details vary.

Infrastructure opportunities are attractive because they serve many use cases. They also tend to be sticky. When a business integrates a system that works, it avoids switching unless there is a major reason. The challenge is that infrastructure must be extremely reliable. Reliability is the product.

Compliance-first products

Compliance-first does not mean "anti-crypto." It means "designed to survive rules." Products that bake compliance into the workflow can win in regulated markets. This includes KYC-friendly onboarding, clear disclosures, robust reporting tools, and conservative risk limits. It also includes consumer protection features, such as scam warnings, transaction confirmations, and permission management.

Compliance-first products can also reduce fraud by making risk signals visible. They can provide users with plain-language explanations of what an approval means. They can reduce accidental losses. This path can build trust, which supports broader adoption. It may be less glamorous, but it can be durable.

Emerging markets use cases

Emerging markets often face real friction in payments, access to global commerce, and currency instability. In some cases, crypto tools can offer alternatives. Remittances and cross-border commerce can improve with better rails. Small businesses can use stablecoin settlement with disciplined workflows. Freelancers can receive global payments faster, though they must manage legal and tax obligations locally.

The key is not to assume one story fits all. Conditions vary. Infrastructure availability varies. Legal risk varies. The opportunity is strongest where local pain is high and where practical access exists. The opportunity is weaker where on-ramps are unreliable, scams are rampant, and legal risk is unclear.

Opportunity Map (one page)

If you want a simple map, use four questions. First, what pain point is clear and measurable. Second, what part of the system reduces that pain reliably. Third, what risks remain, and can they be managed. Fourth, what constraints exist, including regulation, security, and user experience.

Now place opportunities into four lanes. Lane one is "Money rails," which includes stablecoin payments and settlement. Lane two is "Trust rails," which includes custody, identity, and security tooling. Lane three is "Rules rails," which includes compliance-first platforms and reporting systems. Lane four is "Real-world utility," which includes remittances, merchant tools, and industry workflows that reduce friction. When an idea fits a lane and survives the four questions, it is more likely to be real.

Common mistakes

A common mistake is treating opportunity as price appreciation. Another mistake is ignoring compliance and assuming it can be solved later. Another mistake is building tools that are powerful but too complex for normal users. Another mistake is underestimating security requirements for infrastructure. Another mistake is applying one market story to every country. Another mistake is confusing "quiet adoption" with "lack of growth," when it may reflect mature utility.

Quick Check

Can you explain "quiet adoption" as "use without hype."
Can you name two infrastructure opportunities that are not trading-related.
Can you explain why compliance-first products can be a competitive advantage.
Can you name one emerging market use case and one constraint that could block it.
Can you describe the four-question opportunity map in one paragraph.

Part 8 — Future Trends (Practical Forecasting)

Part Introduction: scenarios, not fantasies

The future of crypto is often told as a single story. That is usually a mistake. Industries do not move in one line. They move through cycles of trust, regulation, innovation, and failure. Crypto adds another layer, because it is global software that touches money. That combination creates fast change and unclear outcomes.

This part uses a practical forecasting approach. It separates what is likely from what is uncertain. It also focuses on signals you can observe, not predictions you must believe. Then it offers three scenarios for 2026–2035. These scenarios are not "the answer." They are tools for thinking. Each scenario shows what kinds of products and behaviors survive, and what kinds fail.

The goal is calm readiness. If you understand scenarios, you do not need perfect forecasts. You can build safe habits, choose better tools, and reduce mistakes. You can also avoid the two common traps. The first trap is blind optimism. The second trap is total rejection. A clear view sits between them.

Chapter 21 — Future of Digital Currencies (2026–2035)

Opening

People ask, "What will happen to crypto next." The honest answer is that the future depends on many moving parts. Those parts include regulation, security, user experience, macro conditions, and platform behavior. Some outcomes are more likely than others. Yet uncertainty remains high because laws change, technology evolves, and public trust can shift quickly. This chapter helps you think like a strategist. It shows what seems likely, what remains uncertain, which signals matter, and three scenarios you can use to evaluate any claim about the future.

Definition: practical forecasting in crypto

Practical forecasting means you do not bet on one story. You map a few plausible stories. You watch signals. You update your view when signals change. You focus on what survives across many futures. This approach is useful in crypto because many confident predictions turn out wrong. It is also useful because your main goal is not to be a prophet. Your main goal is to avoid avoidable mistakes.

What is likely vs what is uncertain

Some trends look more likely because they match strong incentives. Incentives are what people do even when excitement fades. One likely trend is deeper integration of compliance into mainstream platforms. This happens because regulated firms need survival, not slogans. Another likely trend is improved user experience over time, because complexity blocks adoption. Another likely trend is continued focus on security, because repeated losses damage trust and invite stricter rules. Another likely trend is the growth of "utility rails," where users care about speed and reliability more than ideology.

Stablecoin use is also likely to remain important, because many users want stable value for transfers and settlement. The exact form and regulatory treatment can vary, but the underlying need is strong. Infrastructure is also likely to grow. Infrastructure includes custody, wallet safety layers, transaction monitoring, and audit-friendly reporting tools. These are not exciting, but they are necessary for large-scale use.

What is uncertain is equally important. It is uncertain how global regulation will converge or fragment. It is uncertain how cross-chain interoperability will evolve and how safe it will become for normal users. It is uncertain how much decentralization will remain in practice, because many users prefer convenience, and convenience often reintroduces central points. It is uncertain how future crises will shape policy responses. It is also uncertain which networks will dominate, because network effects compete with technological change.

It is also uncertain how public trust will shift. Trust can rise slowly and fall quickly. A few major failures can change the whole mood. A few major successes can normalize usage. The direction depends on repeated outcomes, not on one headline.

Key signals to watch

If you want to understand the next decade, watch signals that affect adoption and survival.

Watch regulation signals. Look for clearer licensing paths and clearer boundaries for products. When rules become clearer, serious businesses build more confidently. When rules become harsher or inconsistent, services restrict access and fragmentation grows.

Watch security signals. Look for whether losses are decreasing for ordinary users. Also watch whether wallet experiences become safer by default. If safety improves without requiring expert knowledge, adoption becomes easier.

Watch user experience signals. Look for whether onboarding becomes simpler and whether mistakes become harder to make. When UX improves, scams become less effective, and trust can rise.

Watch stablecoin infrastructure signals. Look for transparency, redemption reliability, and integration with real payment flows. If stablecoins become boring and reliable, that is a sign of maturity.

Watch interoperability signals. Look for safer ways to move value across networks. If cross-chain movement becomes simpler and safer, fragmentation becomes less painful. If it remains risky, users stay trapped in silos or rely on centralized intermediaries.

Watch "real use" signals. Look for use cases that do not depend on price excitement. Examples include merchant settlement, remittances with disciplined workflows, and business treasury operations. When real use grows quietly, the industry becomes less fragile.

3 scenarios for the next decade

Scenario 1: Regulated rails and mainstream normalization
In this scenario, regulation becomes clearer in many major markets. Compliance-first platforms gain share. User protection improves. Stablecoin rails become more common for settlement and cross-border transfers. Innovation continues, but it moves inside clearer boundaries. Many users interact through regulated interfaces. Purely wild products lose reach.

In this scenario, what survives is boring reliability. Secure custody grows. Strong reporting tools grow. Simple wallets grow. Transparent stablecoin systems grow. What struggles is hype-driven projects, fragile mechanisms, and opaque promises. Services that cannot explain risk clearly lose trust faster.

Scenario 2: Fragmented multi-network world with mixed trust

In this scenario, regulation remains uneven across regions. Some markets become strict, others remain flexible, and many remain unclear. Networks multiply. Applications spread across ecosystems. Interoperability improves, but risk remains. Users rely on a mix of centralized and decentralized tools. Adoption grows, but it is uneven. The experience differs sharply by country and by platform.

In this scenario, what survives is flexibility with discipline. Tools that help users manage complexity win. Security layers that reduce mistakes win. Education that teaches simple habits wins. Products that can operate across regions without breaking rules also win. What struggles is anything that needs one global rule set to work everywhere. Anything that depends on smooth cross-chain movement without risk also struggles.

Scenario 3: Trust shocks and "risk-off" consolidation

In this scenario, repeated failures or major security incidents lead to stronger restrictions and a shift toward conservative behavior. Users become cautious. Institutions prefer tightly controlled systems. Retail speculation shrinks for a period. Builders focus on security and compliance. Adoption continues in narrow lanes, but the industry becomes more consolidated.

In this scenario, what survives is strong risk control. Hard security practices become standard. Conservative products gain share. Transparent operations matter more than growth speed. What struggles is fast iteration without audits, aggressive leverage, and systems that rely on constant confidence. The industry becomes smaller in surface area, but stronger in foundations.

What survives in each scenario

Across all three scenarios, a few themes survive.

Security survives, because attackers do not disappear. Compliance capability survives, because rules shape access. Simple user experience survives, because complexity blocks adoption. Stable value transfer tools survive, because payments need stability. Truthful communication survives, because trust is the scarce asset.

Across all three scenarios, a few patterns also fail.

Promises without proof fail, because reality catches up. Business models that rely on confusion fail, because users learn. Systems that cannot handle stress fail, because markets test them. Weak governance fails, because conflicts grow with scale.

Quick Check

Can you explain why scenarios are more useful than one prediction.
Can you name two trends that look likely and one that is uncertain.
Can you name three signals that matter more than price headlines.
Can you describe one scenario in one paragraph without using hype words.
Can you name one survival theme that appears in all scenarios.

Chapter 22 — A Calm Conclusion: How to Stay Smart

Opening

If you remember one idea from this book, remember this. Crypto rewards calm thinking and punishes rushed thinking. It is a system of tools, not a single truth. Some tools are useful. Some tools are dangerous. Your advantage is not secret information. Your advantage is process. Process means you verify, you document, you manage risk, and you avoid emotional decisions. This chapter gives you a simple next-step plan and final checklists you can reuse.

What you should do next

Your next step is not to chase a trend. Your next step is to build a safe base. A safe base includes basic knowledge, safe custody habits, and a repeatable evaluation method. You do not need to learn everything. You need to learn the few things that prevent the biggest mistakes.

Start by choosing your role. Are you mainly a user, a learner, or a market participant. A user needs safe transfer habits. A learner needs a clear mental model and practice. A market participant needs risk control and documentation. One person can be more than one role, but you should separate actions by role so you do not mix goals.

Then choose your boundaries. Boundaries are rules you follow even when you feel excited. A boundary can be "I do not use leverage." Another boundary can be "I do not connect my main wallet to unknown sites." Another boundary can be "I do not act on urgency." Boundaries reduce the need for willpower.

Learning plan (30/60/90 days)

In the next 30 days, focus on foundations and safety.
Read and rewrite key terms in your own words.
Set up basic security habits on your accounts and devices.
Practice small transfers with test amounts to learn workflow.
Create a simple record log for every action you take.

In the next 60 days, focus on evaluation and discipline.
Learn how to read basic project information without excitement.
Practice identifying claims that are not verifiable.
Build your personal checklist for decisions and stick to it.
Study common scam patterns until they feel obvious.

In the next 90 days, focus on controlled exposure and real use.
If you choose to participate, keep exposure small and structured.
Separate wallets by purpose and reduce your blast radius.
Learn one real use case deeply, such as payments workflows.
Review your records and refine your routine for simplicity.

Final checklists (safety + evaluation + discipline)

Safety Checklist
You protect your recovery phrase offline and never share it.
You use strong authentication on custodial accounts.
You verify URLs and avoid random links and urgent messages.
You separate long-term storage from daily-use wallets.
You test small before moving meaningful amounts.
You pause before approvals and reject confusing prompts.

Evaluation Checklist

You can state the problem the project solves in one sentence.
You can explain how it works in plain language.
You can identify who controls key permissions and risks.
You can separate marketing claims from verifiable facts.
You label uncertain areas as Unknown instead of guessing.
You can name the worst-case outcome before taking action.

Discipline Checklist

You avoid urgency and do not act when emotional.
You do not chase returns you cannot explain.
You do not increase risk to recover losses quickly.
You document actions and review them monthly.
You follow your boundaries even when the crowd disagrees.
You accept that doing nothing is sometimes the smart move.

Closing

Crypto will keep changing. Your process can stay stable. When your process is stable, you can learn and adapt without panic. When your process is weak, every market move feels personal. The goal is calm competence. That is how you stay smart in any scenario.

Back Matter

Glossary (A–Z)

This section defines key terms in simple, consistent language. Each term should include a short definition and a short example sentence. Terms should be written for global B1–B2 readers, with minimal jargon.

FAQ

This section answers common questions that readers ask after finishing the book. Questions should focus on clarity and safety. Answers should be educational only and avoid advice. When rules vary by country, the answer should say it depends and encourage local checking.

Templates & Tools

This section provides reusable templates that support disciplined action. Templates should be short, clear, and designed to be copied into notes or spreadsheets.

Project Reality Scorecard

A structured template to evaluate a project without hype. It should cover purpose, users, product proof, governance, risks, and verification steps. It should include an "Unknown" field to prevent guessing.

Security Checklist

A one-page version of the safety habits from Chapter 12. It should be written as short actions a reader can follow every time.

Hype vs Reality Checklist

A pattern-based list that helps readers identify persuasion tactics, weak claims, urgency traps, and missing evidence. It should focus on behavior signals rather than complex technical analysis.

Further Reading

A curated list of recommended reading categories, not a promise of "latest." Categories can include basic blockchain concepts, risk management, security hygiene, financial regulation basics, and trustworthy technical documentation.

Index (optional)

An index can help print readers find terms and topics quickly. It is optional, but it improves usability for reference-style reading.

Mini Glossary — 120 Essential Crypto Terms (Term — Definition)

Address — A public identifier used to receive crypto. It is like an account number on a network.

Airdrop — A token distribution to many wallets. It is often used for marketing or community rewards.

Algorithmic Stablecoin — A stablecoin that tries to hold a peg using rules and incentives. It can fail if demand collapses.

All-Time High (ATH) — The highest recorded price of an asset. It is a historical reference point only.

Altcoin — Any cryptocurrency that is not Bitcoin. The term is informal.

AML (Anti-Money Laundering) — Policies that aim to prevent illegal money movement. Crypto services often must follow AML rules.

AMM (Automated Market Maker) — A system that lets users trade using liquidity pools. Prices move by formulas, not order books.

API (Application Programming Interface) — A controlled way for software to connect and exchange data. Exchanges often provide APIs for trading tools.

Arbitrage — Buying in one place and selling in another to use price differences. It can reduce price gaps across markets.

ASIC Miner — A specialized machine designed for mining. It is built for a specific algorithm.

Asset Custody — The process of holding and protecting assets. Custody can be self-managed or done by a provider.

Attack Surface — All the points where a system can be attacked. More complexity usually increases attack surface.

Audit (Smart Contract) — A review of code for security issues. An audit lowers risk but never removes it.

Bagholder — A person holding an asset after a sharp fall. The term is slang and often negative.

Bear Market — A long period of falling prices and weak sentiment. It usually reduces risk-taking.

Benchmark — A reference used to compare performance. In crypto, it can be a major asset or index.

Bid-Ask Spread — The gap between the best buy price and best sell price. A smaller spread often means better liquidity.

Bitcoin — The first widely adopted cryptocurrency. It introduced a decentralized payment network.

Block — A batch of transactions added to a blockchain. It becomes part of the permanent record.

Block Explorer — A website or tool to view blockchain transactions and addresses. It helps verify activity publicly.

Block Height — The number of blocks from the first block to the current one. It is a simple measure of chain progress.

Block Reward — The reward given to validators or miners for adding a block. It can include fees and new coins.

Blockchain — A shared ledger that records transactions in blocks. Many nodes keep copies for verification.

Bridge — A system that moves assets or data between blockchains. Bridges can be high risk targets.

Burn — Permanently removing tokens from supply. It is done by sending tokens to an unusable address.

CEX (Centralized Exchange) — A company-run exchange that holds accounts and matches trades. Users rely on the platform's controls.

Chain — A shorthand for a blockchain network. People use it to describe where assets live.

Chain Reorg (Reorganization) — A change in recent blocks due to competing histories. It can reverse recent transactions temporarily.

Cold Storage — Keeping keys offline to reduce hacking risk. It improves security but adds handling complexity.

Collateral — An asset locked to secure a loan or position. If value drops, liquidation may happen.

Compliance — Following laws, rules, and internal policies. It often includes identity checks and reporting.

Confirmation — A sign that a transaction is included in a block. More confirmations can reduce reversal risk.

Consensus — How a network agrees on the valid ledger state. It prevents double spending.

Consensus Algorithm — The method used to reach consensus. Examples include Proof of Work and Proof of Stake.

Contract Address — The address of a smart contract on a chain. It is used to interact with the contract.

Cross-Chain — Involving more than one blockchain. Cross-chain systems often rely on bridges or messaging.

Cryptography — Math techniques used to secure data and prove ownership. Crypto networks use it for signatures and hashing.

Custodial Wallet — A wallet where a service holds your keys. You gain convenience but accept platform risk.

DAO (Decentralized Autonomous Organization) — A group coordinated by on-chain rules and voting. Real-world control still matters.

dApp (Decentralized Application) — An app that uses blockchain for parts of its logic. It often relies on smart contracts.

DeFi (Decentralized Finance) — Financial services built on smart contracts. It includes trading, lending, and staking products.

Depeg — When a stablecoin moves away from its target price. Depegs can be temporary or permanent.

Decentralization — Distributing control across many participants. It reduces single points of failure, but trade-offs exist.

Derivatives — Contracts whose value depends on an underlying asset. Examples include futures and options.

DEX (Decentralized Exchange) — A trading platform built with smart contracts. Users trade from their own wallets.

Difficulty (Mining) — A measure that adjusts how hard it is to mine blocks. It helps keep block timing stable.

Distributed Ledger — A ledger stored across multiple nodes. Blockchain is one type of distributed ledger.

Double Spend — Trying to spend the same coins twice. Consensus rules are designed to prevent this.

Dust (Dusting) — Very small amounts of crypto sent to many addresses. It can be used for tracking attempts.

EIP (Ethereum Improvement Proposal) — A proposal process to change Ethereum standards. It documents and debates changes.

Encryption — Protecting data so only authorized parties can read it. Wallets may encrypt local key files.

Entropy — The randomness used to create secure keys. Low entropy can create weak security.

ERC-20 — A common token standard on Ethereum. It defines basic token behavior.

ERC-721 — A standard for unique tokens, often used for NFTs. Each token has distinct identity.

Escrow — Holding funds until conditions are met. Smart contracts can provide automated escrow.

Ethereum — A blockchain known for smart contracts. It supports many tokens and dApps.

Exchange Rate — The price between two assets. Rates can vary across platforms and time.

Exit Liquidity — Buyers who enter late and fund others' profits. It is a warning concept, not a rule.

Faucet — A tool that gives small test tokens for learning. It is common on test networks.

Fee Market — The system that sets transaction fees based on demand. High demand often raises fees.

Fiat — Government-issued money like USD or EUR. Crypto prices are often quoted in fiat.

Finality — The point when a transaction is very hard to reverse. Different chains have different finality models.

Flash Loan — A loan that must be repaid within one transaction. It enables complex strategies and attacks.

Fork — A change in protocol rules that splits a chain or upgrades it. Forks can be planned or disputed.

Front-Running — Placing trades ahead of others based on order knowledge. It can happen in mempools and some markets.

FUD — Fear, uncertainty, and doubt. It describes negative sentiment, sometimes used unfairly.

Futures — A contract to buy or sell later at an agreed condition. It is used for hedging or speculation.

Gas — The unit for computation cost on Ethereum-like chains. Users pay gas fees to run transactions.

Genesis Block — The first block of a blockchain. It starts the chain history.

Governance — How decisions are made about protocol changes. It can be on-chain, off-chain, or mixed.

Hard Fork — A rule change that is not compatible with old rules. Nodes must upgrade or split occurs.

Hash — A fixed-length output from data using a hashing function. It helps verify integrity quickly.

Hash Rate — The total computing power used for mining on a network. It is often linked to security in PoW chains.

HODL — Slang for holding long-term. It is a community term, not a strategy guarantee.

Hot Wallet — A wallet connected to the internet. It is convenient but easier to attack.

IDO (Initial DEX Offering) — A token sale done through a decentralized platform. Risks can be high.

IEO (Initial Exchange Offering) — A token sale hosted by an exchange. The exchange may screen projects, but risk remains.

Inflation (Token Supply) — An increase in token supply over time. It can affect value if demand does not grow.

Interoperability — The ability of different chains or apps to work together. It reduces ecosystem fragmentation.

KYC (Know Your Customer) — Identity checks required by many regulated platforms. It is common on centralized exchanges.

Layer 1 (L1) — The base blockchain network. It handles core security and settlement.

Layer 2 (L2) — A system built on top of L1 to improve speed or cost. It often posts results back to L1.

Ledger (On-Chain) — The recorded history of transactions. On a public chain, it is visible to everyone.

Leverage — Borrowing to increase position size. It increases both potential gains and losses.

Liquidity — How easily an asset can be bought or sold without moving price much. Low liquidity increases slippage.

Liquidity Pool — Funds locked in a pool for trading or lending. Providers earn fees but face risks.

Liquidation — Forced closing of a position when collateral is too low. It is common in lending and margin trading.

Market Cap — Price multiplied by circulating supply. It is a rough size measure, not a full valuation.

Mempool — A waiting area for unconfirmed transactions. Congestion here can raise fees.

MEV (Maximal Extractable Value) — Profit from ordering or including transactions. It affects fairness and cost.

Mint — Creating new tokens, often by a contract rule. NFTs are also minted as new unique items.

Multisig (Multi-Signature) — A wallet that needs multiple approvals to spend. It reduces single-key risk.

NFT (Non-Fungible Token) — A unique token representing a specific item or right. Ownership and utility depend on the project.

Node — A computer running the network software. Nodes help verify and distribute data.

Nonce — A value used once for security or mining puzzles. It helps prevent replay and supports hashing.

Off-Ramp — Converting crypto back into fiat. This often happens through exchanges or payment services.

On-Ramp — Converting fiat into crypto. This often involves regulated providers.

Oracle — A service that brings external data to smart contracts. Bad oracle data can break contracts.

Order Book — A list of buy and sell orders on an exchange. It determines prices through matching.

OTC (Over-the-Counter) — Trading directly between parties, not on a public order book. It can reduce market impact.

Permissionless — Open to anyone without approval. Many public blockchains are permissionless.

Permissioned — Access requires approval or membership. Some enterprise chains use this model.

Private Key — A secret that proves control of funds. Losing it can mean losing access permanently.

Public Key — A key used to verify signatures. It is linked to addresses in many systems.

Proof of Work (PoW) — Consensus using computation to secure the chain. Mining is the process used in PoW.

Proof of Stake (PoS) — Consensus using staked assets to select validators. Slashing may punish bad behavior.

Protocol — The set of rules a network follows. Changes to the protocol affect everyone.

Rug Pull — A scam where insiders drain liquidity or abandon a project. It often happens in new tokens.

Seed Phrase (Recovery Phrase) — A set of words that can restore a wallet. Anyone with it can control the funds.

Self-Custody — Holding your own keys without a custodian. It increases control and responsibility.

Settlement — Final recording of transfers and balances. In crypto, settlement happens on-chain.

Sharding — Splitting data processing across parts of a network. It aims to improve scalability.

Signature (Digital Signature) — Proof that a message was authorized by a private key. It secures transactions.

Slashing — A penalty in some PoS systems. It can reduce a validator's stake for misbehavior.

Slippage — The difference between expected price and actual execution price. It increases with low liquidity.

Smart Contract — Code that runs on a blockchain. It can automate rules and transfers.

Stablecoin — A token designed to stay near a reference value. Stability depends on reserves or mechanisms.

Staking — Locking assets to help secure a network or earn rewards. Rules and risks depend on the chain.

Tokenomics — How a token's supply, distribution, and incentives work. Bad tokenomics can damage a project.

Volatility — How quickly prices move up and down. High volatility increases risk for users and traders.

www.ingramcontent.com/pod-product-compliance
Lightning Source LLC
Chambersburg PA
CBHW050311230526
45471CB00005B/2120